TIME TRAVELING TO
1975
CELEBRATING A SPECIAL YEAR

TIME TRAVELING TO 1975

Author
Alex J. Harper

Design
Gonçalo Sousa

November 2024
ISBN: 9798345632307

Surprise!

Dear reader, thank you so much for purchasing my book!

To make this book more (much more!) affordable, the images are all black & white, but I've created a special gift for you!

You can now have access, for FREE, to the PDF version of this book with the original images!

Keep in mind that some are originally black and white, but some are colored.

Go to page 101 and follow the instructions to download it.

I hope you enjoy it!

Contents

JAWS

Chapter I: News & Current Events 1975

Leading Events

Thatcher Triumphs: UK Conservative Leader Elected - February 11th

"The Iron Lady"

In a stunning political twist, Margaret Thatcher, a relatively unknown figure to the public, rose from underdog status to become the first woman ever to lead a major political party in Britain. Edward Heath, who had been the Conservative Party leader for a decade and even served as Prime Minister, called for a leadership election to solidify his position. However, discontent brewed within the party after multiple electoral failures under his leadership. Despite strong support from the Conservative establishment and media, Heath faced an unexpected challenger in the form of Thatcher, whose campaign was managed by Airey Neave.

As the ballots were cast, the first round produced a shockwave-Thatcher had edged out Heath, though not by enough to clinch the victory outright. Heath, shaken by the results, withdrew from the race, leading to a second ballot. In a decisive moment, Thatcher triumphed over her closest rival, William Whitelaw, securing her leadership. This event marked the beginning of a new era for the Conservative Party, as the once underestimated Margaret Thatcher would soon carve out her place as a pivotal figure in British history. The political landscape had been reshaped, with Thatcher on the verge of becoming the "Iron Lady."

Microsoft's Genesis: Gates and Allen Found Tech Giant - April 4th

In a moment that would forever change the tech world, two young, ambitious friends, Bill Gates and Paul Allen, embarked on an extraordinary journey. Inspired by the Altair 8800, the first-ever microcomputer, Allen spotted its potential in

Microsoft's Genesis: Allen and Gates

a magazine and hurried to show it to Gates. The duo, fueled by excitement, decided to develop a BASIC interpreter for the machine. Remarkably, they succeeded, despite not even having an Altair to test it on. Their success caught the eye of Altair's manufacturer, MITS, leading to an agreement that set the stage for the future giant they would soon create.

1978 photo of early Microsoft employees

With this momentum, Gates and Allen co-founded a company they called "Micro-Soft" in Albuquerque. Their vision was to bring computing to the masses by focusing on both software and hardware. As their company grew, they recruited a handful of dedicated employees and expanded internationally. The venture took off when they moved to Washington, and Microsoft began to dominate the software landscape. Little did anyone know that these two childhood friends would eventually transform the world of personal computing, building a legacy that would shape technology for generations to come. What started as a bold idea would become one of the most influential companies in history.

Former Vietnam President Duong Van Minh (center, looking down) leaves the presidential palace

Saigon Falls: The Vietnam War Ends - April 30th

In a dramatic and chaotic finale, the Vietnam War came to an unforgettable conclusion as the capital of South Vietnam, Saigon, fell to the North Vietnamese forces. The final assault began with intense artillery bombardment, overwhelming the South Vietnamese defenders. By the next day, North Vietnamese troops, led by General Văn Tiên Dũng, had taken control of key areas in the city. The moment that symbolized the end came when the flag of the North was raised over the presidential palace, signaling the collapse of the South Vietnamese regime.

Amid the chaos, Operation Frequent Wind saw the largest helicopter evacuation in history, as tens of thousands of South Vietnamese civilians and

Communist troops advance toward the center of Saigon

almost all remaining U.S. personnel were airlifted out. Many feared for their lives as the communist forces swept in, while a few Americans chose to stay behind. The U.S. military, long gone from combat, could only watch from afar as Saigon was engulfed in the final stages of the war. In the aftermath, Saigon was renamed Ho Chi Minh City in honor of North Vietnam's revolutionary leader, though many locals continued to call it Saigon.

Apollo-Soyuz: Historic Space Docking - July 17th

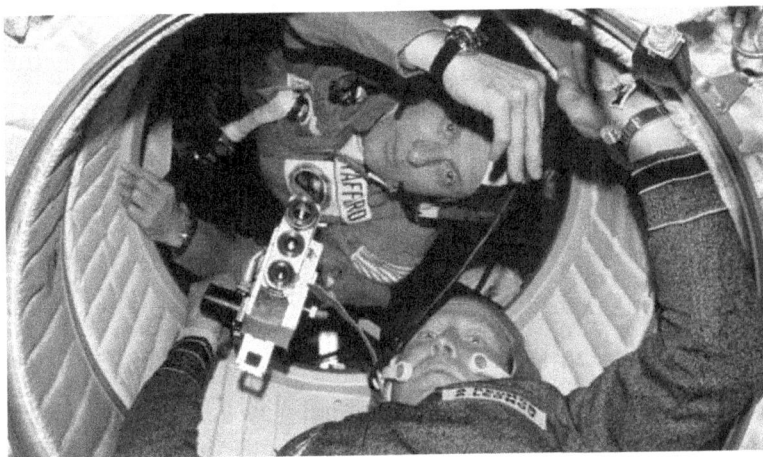

Stafford and Leonov

In an extraordinary display of Cold War détente, American and Soviet space crews came together for the first-ever international space mission. The Apollo-Soyuz Test Project brought together two rival nations in a historic docking between an American Apollo spacecraft and a Soviet Soyuz capsule. Millions of viewers around the world watched as astronauts Thomas Stafford, Vance Brand, and Deke Slayton joined cosmonauts Alexei Leonov and Valery Kubasov in a handshake that symbolized a moment of

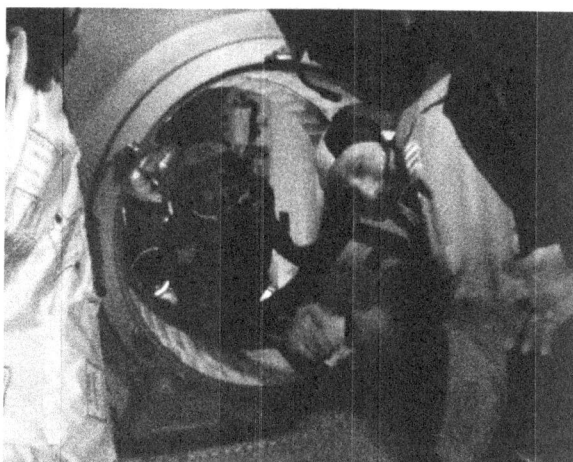

The historic handshake between Stafford and Leono

unity between the superpowers. During the mission, the crews conducted joint and individual experiments, including an ingenious solar eclipse created by the Apollo module to allow the Soyuz crew to capture images of the solar corona. This collaboration provided invaluable engineering experience for future international missions like the Shuttle-Mir program and the International Space Station. Apollo-Soyuz marked the final flight of an Apollo spacecraft and also became the last American crewed spaceflight for nearly six years, until the Space Shuttle era began. The mission was a testament to what could be achieved through cooperation, even in times of political tension, leaving a lasting legacy of peace and partnership in space exploration.

Banqiao Dam Disaster: China's Devastating Floods - August 8th

In one of the deadliest disasters of the 20th century, the collapse of the Banqiao Dam in China unleashed a catastrophic flood that devastated millions. Triggered by Typhoon Nina, the dam–along with 61 others in Henan Province–was overwhelmed by record-breaking rainfall. The sheer force of the floodwaters swept through the region, affecting over 10 million people and submerging an area of 12,000 square kilometers. Entire cities and villages were destroyed, with millions of homes washed away and the death toll ranging from tens of thousands to nearly a quarter-million. The Banqiao Dam had been built during China's Great Leap Forward

A view of Banqiao Dam after its collapse

with Soviet assistance, but design flaws and a focus on water retention rather than flood control left it vulnerable. When more than a year's worth of rain fell in a single day, the dam's defenses crumbled, releasing a wall of water that wiped out everything in its path.

For decades, details of the disaster were concealed, only coming to light in the 1990s, and officially declassified years later. The collapse not only exposed flaws in China's dam construction policies but also the environmental mismanagement of the time. Even today, it stands as a somber reminder of the devastating power of nature—and human error.

Other Major Events

Watergate Scandal: Culprits Found Guilty - January 1st

The Watergate scandal, one of the most notorious political controversies in U.S. history, reached a dramatic conclusion with the conviction of several high-ranking officials in Richard Nixon's administration. It all began with the 1972 break-in at the Democratic National Committee headquarters, orchestrated by members of Nixon's re-election team. As investigations

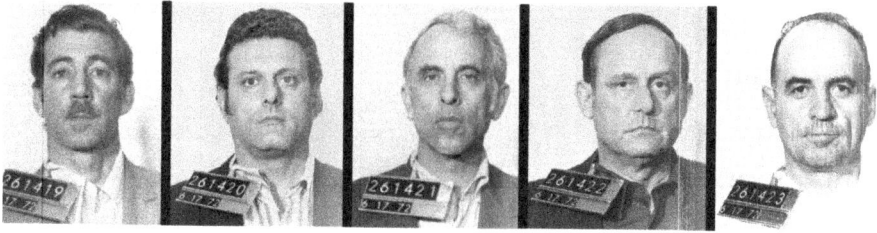

Five burglary suspects accused of attempting to bug DNC headquarters and steal documents

unfolded, it was revealed that the president and his aides had attempted to cover up their involvement. The televised Senate hearings captivated the nation, and mounting evidence, including secret Oval Office tapes, proved Nixon's complicity.

Nixon announces his resignation

The scandal culminated in Nixon's resignation, making him the only U.S. president to step down from office. Eventually, key figures such as H.R. Haldeman, John Ehrlichman, and John Mitchell were found guilty. Watergate led to sweeping political and legal reforms, while also tarnishing the reputation of the legal profession, as many involved were attorneys. It forever changed the American political landscape and public trust in government.

Haicheng Earthquake: First Predicted Quake - February 4th

In a remarkable event, the city of Haicheng, China, became the site of the first-ever predicted earthquake, saving thousands of lives. Hours before a massive 7.5-magnitude quake struck, authorities ordered an unprecedented evacuation, driven by the detection of a pronounced foreshock sequence. This rapid response is credited with reducing fatalities, as much of the city's population had already fled. However, despite the successful

The location where the Haicheng earthquake took place

evacuation, the harsh winter took its toll. Many evacuees, forced to live in makeshift shelters, succumbed to hypothermia or frostbite, while fires caused by heating and cooking claimed additional lives. Although the prediction was celebrated, it later came under scrutiny, with some experts labeling it a fluke.

The evacuation was a rare success, limiting the death toll to under 2,500. Without it, experts estimate that over 150,000 people could have been injured. The Haicheng earthquake remains a pivotal moment in the history of disaster preparedness, though its scientific basis remains debated.

Helsinki Accords: A Step Toward Peace - August 1st

The Helsinki Accords marked a significant moment in Cold War diplomacy, bringing together 35 nations–including the United States, the Soviet Union, and almost all European countries–in an effort to ease tensions between East and West. The agreement aimed to improve cooperation on security, economic, and human rights issues, but was not legally binding, as it lacked treaty status. While the Soviets viewed the accords as a diplomatic victory, especially with the recognition of post-World War II borders, Western

Helmut Schmidt, Erich Honecker, Gerald Ford, and Bruno Kreisky at the Helsinki Accords

nations focused on the human rights provisions. These human rights clauses would later inspire movements advocating for greater freedom in Soviet-controlled regions. The formation of Helsinki Watch, which evolved into Human Rights Watch, demonstrated how the accords became a tool for promoting civil liberties. Though the agreement solidified Cold War boundaries, it also planted the seeds for future challenges to authoritarian regimes in Eastern Europe, making the Helsinki Accords a complex but important step toward peace.

Portuguese troops on patrol in Angola

Angola's Struggle: Independence and Civil War - November 11th

Angola's long-awaited independence from Portugal quickly descended into chaos as a brutal civil war erupted between rival factions. The two main groups, the communist MPLA and the anti-communist

UNITA, both former allies in the fight for freedom, now clashed in a fierce struggle for power. With external forces heavily involved, the conflict became a Cold War battleground, as the Soviet Union and Cuba backed the MPLA, while the U.S. and South Africa supported UNITA.

The fighting, which spanned nearly three decades, devastated the nation. Entire cities were destroyed, the economy collapsed, and hundreds of thousands of lives were lost. Over a million people were displaced as the violence ravaged the country's infrastructure. The war's end in 2002 left Angola in ruins, and land mines from the conflict continue to cause civilian casualties. Despite the horrors, Angola's independence marked a turning point in African history, though peace came at a tremendous cost.

The delegates at the OPEC meeting

OPEC Attack: Terror Strikes Headquarters - December 21st

In a bold and chilling attack, six terrorists stormed the OPEC headquarters in Vienna, taking more than 60 hostages during a high-profile meeting of oil leaders. Led by the infamous Carlos the Jackal, the attackers killed three individuals, including an Austrian policeman and a Libyan economist. The group, calling themselves the "Arm of the Arab Revolution," demanded political recognition and aimed to send a violent message to the global community. The tense standoff resulted in complex diplomatic negotiations that unfolded over two days. The terrorists and hostages were flown to Algiers and Tripoli, where the ordeal ended with no further bloodshed, as all hostages and terrorists were released. The attack was one of the first times Arab states were targeted by terrorism, prompting increased cooperation among them to combat future threats. Carlos the Jackal later faced justice, and the event remains a significant episode in the history of international terrorism.

Political Events

Operation Babylift: Vietnamese Orphans Evacuated - April 4th

As the Vietnam War neared its devastating conclusion, Operation Babylift became a lifeline for thousands of Vietnamese orphans. Announced by President Gerald Ford, the mission aimed to evacuate about 2,000 orphans from Saigon to safety. Amidst growing fears

Babies secured in seatbelted boxes on a plane during Operation Babylift

of the fall of the city, American and South Vietnamese personnel worked tirelessly to carry out this massive humanitarian effort.

Tragically, one of the first planes involved in the operation, a Lockheed C-5 Galaxy, crashed, killing 155 passengers, including many children. Despite this heartbreaking setback, the evacuation continued, and over 2,500 orphans were safely relocated. The operation was part of a larger effort to evacuate refugees, including Operation New Life, which rescued over 110,000 Vietnamese civilians.

Operation Babylift remains a poignant chapter in the final days of the Vietnam War, symbolizing both the chaos of war and the hope for a new beginning for the orphans whose lives were forever changed by this daring mission.

Gandhi Convicted: Electoral Corruption Exposed - June 12th

Justice Jagmohanlal Sinha convicted Indira Gandhi of electoral malpractice

In a landmark ruling, India's Prime Minister Indira Gandhi was found guilty of electoral malpractices by the Allahabad High Court, creating a major political crisis. The court ruled that Gandhi had used government resources and officials to secure her re-election in 1971, thus invalidating her victory and barring her from holding office for six years. The ruling galvanized opposition parties, led by Jayaprakash Narayan, who demanded Gandhi's resignation and called for civil disobedience.

Instead of stepping down, Gandhi declared a state of emergency, citing national security concerns. This move allowed her to arrest opposition leaders, censor the press, and postpone elections. During this period, her government also amended the Constitution to protect her position. However, when elections were finally held in 1977, Gandhi's party suffered a crushing defeat, and Raj Narain, the man who had filed the case, beat her in Rae Bareilly, ending her reign as Prime Minister, at least temporarily.

Papua New Guinea: Independence Achieved - September 16th

Prince Charles at Independence Day ceremonies in Papua New Guinea

Papua New Guinea's path to independence was shaped by decades of foreign control, first divided between German and British powers and later governed by Australia after World War I. With growing calls for self-governance, especially from indigenous groups like the Tolai people, pressure mounted for autonomy. In the early 1970s, Australian Prime Minister Gough Whitlam supported the transition, and Michael Somare became the first Papua New Guinean Chief Minister.

In a landmark moment, Papua New Guinea achieved full independence, with Whitlam and Prince Charles attending the official ceremony. Michael Somare continued as the nation's first Prime Minister. Known for its remarkable linguistic diversity and rural population, Papua New Guinea transitioned from colonial rule to becoming an independent member of the Commonwealth of Nations. This independence marked the first and only time Australia granted independence to a former colony, setting a new chapter in the country's history.

Juan Carlos Crowned: Spain's New King - November 22nd

The coronation of Juan Carlos I marked a pivotal moment in Spain's history, as he assumed the role of king following the death of dictator Francisco Franco. Initially seen as a continuation of Franco's legacy, Juan Carlos quickly

Proclamation of Juan Carlos as king at the Palacio de las Cortes

surprised many by steering Spain toward democracy. He replaced the conservative Carlos Arias Navarro with reformist Adolfo Suárez, who led the country through a peaceful transition. In 1976, the Political Reform Act paved the way for free elections, overcoming resistance from Francoist factions. By 1978, Spain had a new democratic constitution, and in 1981, Juan Carlos played a critical role in thwarting an attempted military coup, solidifying his reputation as a defender of democracy.

Over the following decades, Spain saw political stability and economic growth, transitioning from dictatorship to a modern European democracy. Juan Carlos' reign, though ending in 2014 amid personal and political challenges, was marked by his crucial role in shaping a democratic Spain.

Other Notable Events

Australia's Color TV Debut - March 1st

Australia's television landscape changed forever with the official debut of color broadcasts. After years of anticipation, all TV stations switched to color, though some had been conducting experimental broadcasts since the previous year. The transition came with a hefty price tag, with the ABC and commercial networks investing millions in new equipment.

Viewers eager to experience the new technology had to purchase color

TV sets, sparking a rapid uptake. By 1978, the majority of households in major cities had made the switch. Advertisers, initially hesitant due to the higher cost of color commercials, soon realized the

At midnight on 1 March 1975, Aunty Jack, Thin Arthur, and Kid Eager faced the 'color monster' on ABC in a unique showdown

impact of vibrant visuals, especially as color TV revolutionized how products were showcased. The transition was one of the fastest in the world, with color television quickly becoming the norm across Australia, transforming how people experienced entertainment and events, including the iconic Melbourne Cup.

Junko Tabei on top of Mount Everest, 1975

First Woman on Everest: Tabei's Triumph - May 16th

Junko Tabei made history as the first woman to conquer Mount Everest, defying societal expectations and immense physical challenges. Leading a 15-member all-female Japanese expedition, Tabei and her team faced numerous obstacles, including an avalanche that temporarily buried her and several others. Despite injuries, she pressed on, eventually reaching the summit with her sherpa guide, Ang Tsering. Tabei's ascent was groundbreaking not only for her personal achievement but also as a symbol of perseverance in the face of adversity. Her triumph earned her international acclaim, with celebrations held in both Nepal and Japan. However, Tabei, known for her humility, downplayed the fame, expressing that she never sought to be the "first woman," but simply the 36th person to reach Everest's peak. Her legacy extends far beyond Everest, with Tabei becoming a global advocate for the environment and inspiring future generations.

Mandelbrot's Insight: "Fractal" Coined - 1975 (Exact Date Unknown)

In a groundbreaking moment for mathematics, Benoît Mandelbrot coined the term "fractal" to describe complex geometric shapes that exhibit self-similarity at every scale. These structures, like jagged coastlines or the intricate leaves of ferns, reveal that what appears chaotic in nature often holds a hidden, repeating order. Mandelbrot's pioneering work in fractal geometry challenged traditional ideas of geometry, showing that seemingly irregular forms in nature could be understood through simple mathematical rules.

Benoît Mandelbrot

Mandelbrot's discovery, detailed in his book *Les Objets Fractals*, revolutionized fields ranging from physics and meteorology to economics and computer graphics. With the help of early computer graphics at IBM, Mandelbrot visualized fractals, including his now-famous Mandelbrot

The Mandelbrot set within a continuously colored environment

set. His insights opened up new ways of understanding the complexity in natural phenomena, forever changing how we perceive and study the world around us.

Hoffa Vanishes: The Mysterious Disappearance - July 30th

On a summer afternoon, labor leader Jimmy Hoffa vanished without a trace after arriving for a meeting with Mafia-linked figures at a restaurant near Detroit. Known for his powerful influence as the president of the Teamsters Union and his ties to organized crime, Hoffa was seeking to regain control of the union following his release from prison. After waiting in the parking lot and making several frustrated phone calls, Hoffa was last seen near his car, but never returned home.

His disappearance sparked widespread speculation and investigations, with many believing he was murdered by the Mafia. Despite extensive searches and countless theories, Hoffa's body was never found, and the case remains

James R. Hoffa

one of the most enduring mysteries in U.S. history. He was declared legally dead in 1982, but the circumstances surrounding his disappearance continue to captivate the public to this day.

WGPR-TV 62: First African American Owned Station - September 29th

WGPR-TV 62 made history as the first African American-owned television station in the U.S., broadcasting from Detroit. Spearheaded by William V. Banks and supported by community leaders, the station was created to address the lack of representation in mainstream media. Banks, a son of Kentucky sharecroppers, envisioned WGPR as a platform for Black voices and talent, offering opportunities in television production, journalism, and sales.

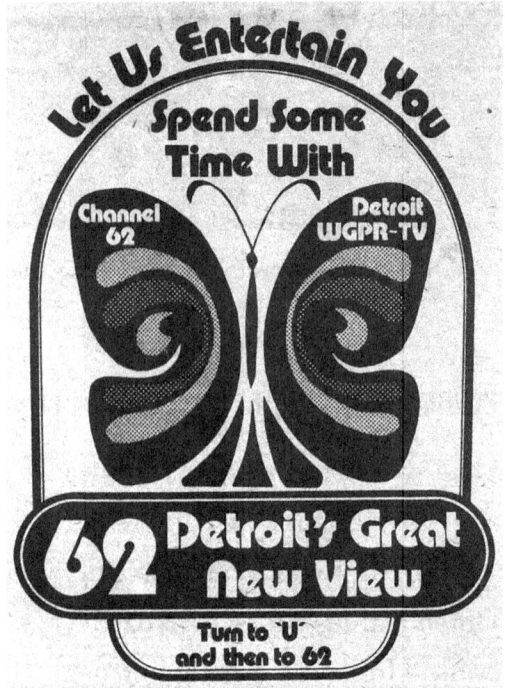

Print ad for WGPR-TV featuring its distinctive 'butterfly' logo

The station's early programming featured the groundbreaking "Big City News," the first Black prime-time news team, and the popular dance show "The Scene." President Gerald Ford congratulated the station, recognizing it as a symbol of Black enterprise and progress.

Though WGPR-TV was later sold to CBS in 1995, its legacy continues through the William V. Banks Broadcast Museum, which celebrates the station's pioneering role in media and African American history.

Chapter II: Crime & Punishment 1975

Madagascar's President Assassinated - February 11th

Colonel Richard Ratsimandrava

Colonel Richard Ratsimandrava's tenure as President of Madagascar was tragically brief. A decorated soldier and politician, Ratsimandrava had risen through the ranks after Madagascar gained independence from France. In 1972, he was appointed Minister of the Interior under a military government, and by early 1975, he succeeded President Gabriel Ramanantsoa. However, just six days into his presidency, Ratsimandrava was assassinated while driving home from the presidential palace, plunging the nation into political chaos.

The assassination was blamed on members of the Republican Security Forces, a group disbanded by his predecessor. His death threatened to ignite a civil war, with tensions rising between the military government and supporters of former President Philibert Tsiranana. The assassination remains a dark chapter in Madagascar's history, and on its 31st anniversary, the nation reflected on his brief rule and the impact of his tragic death.

King Faisal: Assassinated by Nephew - March 25th

King Faisal of Saudi Arabia, known for his modernization efforts and firm stance on international issues, was assassinated by his nephew, Prince Faisal bin Musaid, during a routine majlis–a traditional gathering where citizens petition the king. The shocking incident unfolded when the young prince approached the king for a customary embrace, only to pull out a pistol and shoot him at

King Faisal

point-blank range. Despite efforts to save his life, King Faisal succumbed to his injuries shortly after being rushed to the hospital.

The assassination was believed to be an act of revenge, possibly linked to the death of the assassin's brother, who was killed in 1966 during protests

Funeral of King Faisal

against the king's introduction of television. The assassination sent shockwaves throughout the kingdom, and Prince Faisal was later executed for regicide. King Faisal's death marked the end of a reign that had left a lasting impact on Saudi Arabia's modernization and its place on the global stage.

Fromme's Attempt: President Ford Targeted - September 5th

On a quiet September day in Sacramento, Lynette "Squeaky" Fromme, a devoted follower of the notorious Manson Family, attempted to assassinate President Gerald Ford during his visit to Sacramento. On a public walkway near the California State Capitol, Fromme, dressed in red, approached Ford and pointed a Colt .45 pistol

Secret Service shields President Gerald Ford after the assassination attempt

at him from just two feet away. However, the gun failed to fire, as she had not chambered a round.

Secret Service agent Larry Buendorf quickly intervened, disarming Fromme and taking her into custody. Ford, unharmed and remarkably calm, continued

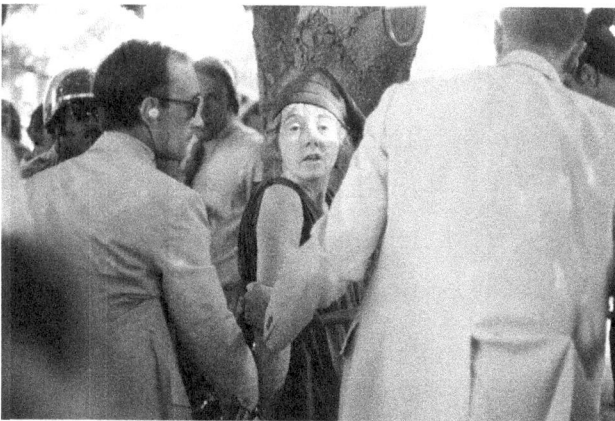

Secret Service agents handcuff Lynette 'Squeaky' Fromme after she aimed at President Gerald Ford

with his schedule, meeting with California Governor Jerry Brown shortly after the attempt. Fromme claimed her motivation was to protest environmental damage, particularly its impact on air, trees, water, and animals (ATWA). She was sentenced to life in prison but was released in 2009 after serving 34 years. The assassination attempt highlighted both the lasting influence of the Manson Family and the vulnerabilities in presidential security.

Spain's Final Executions: Five ETA and FRAP Members - September 27th

Spain's final executions occurred during the last months of Francisco Franco's dictatorship, when two members of the Basque separatist group ETA and three members of the Revolutionary Antifascist Patriotic Front (FRAP) were sentenced to death by military tribunals. They were convicted of killing policemen and civil guards, and their execution by firing squad sparked widespread international outrage and diplomatic protests.

Francisco Franco

Demonstrations erupted across Europe, with many criticizing Spain's flawed judicial process and Franco's authoritarian rule. The Pope and various foreign leaders called for clemency, but their pleas were ignored. These executions marked the end of capital punishment in Spain, as no more took place following Franco's death two months later.

ETA members training in the Basque Country

The events intensified global condemnation of Franco's regime, already isolated for its ties to fascism and post-war repression. By 1978, Spain's new constitution largely abolished the death penalty, with final restrictions removed in 1995.

Chapter III: Entertainment 1975

Silver Screen

Top Film of 1975: Jaws

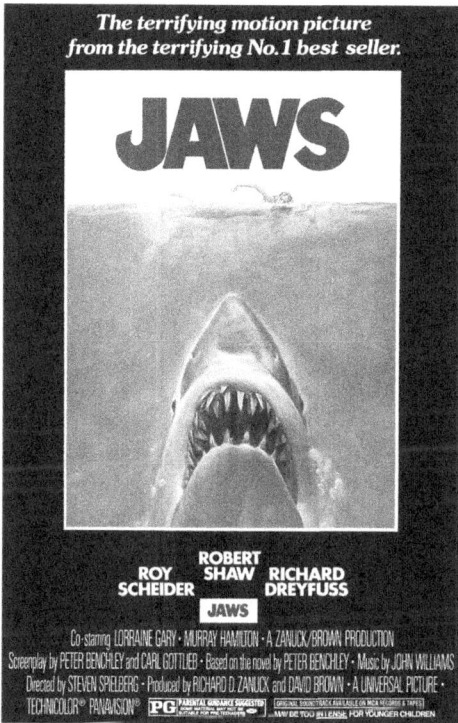

Jaws

"Jaws", directed by Steven Spielberg and based on Peter Benchley's novel, became the top film of 1975 and the first true summer blockbuster. The film follows police chief Martin Brody (Roy Scheider), a marine biologist (Richard Dreyfuss), and a shark hunter (Robert Shaw) as they attempt to catch a man-eating great white shark terrorizing the coastal town of Amity Island. The production was fraught with difficulties, as malfunctioning mechanical sharks forced Spielberg to suggest the shark's presence through ominous music by John Williams, adding suspense that drew comparisons to Alfred Hitchcock. Despite its troubled production, Jaws shattered box-office records, grossing over $100 million and becoming the highest-grossing film of all time until "Star Wars". The film's success was propelled by an innovative marketing campaign and its wide summer release, a first for major studio pictures. It also won multiple awards, including an Oscar for its iconic score. "Jaws" transformed the film industry, establishing the summer blockbuster model and influencing many thrillers to come.

Although some critics initially dismissed the film for its mechanical shark and exploitative violence, it is now recognized as a cinematic classic, preserved in the National Film Registry for its cultural and historical significance.

Remaining Top 3

One Flew Over the Cuckoo's Nest

One Flew Over the Cuckoo's Nest

"One Flew Over the Cuckoo's Nest" (1975), directed by Miloš Forman and based on Ken Kesey's novel, stars Jack Nicholson as Randle McMurphy, a rebellious patient in a mental institution controlled by the tyrannical Nurse Ratched (Louise Fletcher). The film, featuring a talented cast including Danny DeVito, Will Sampson, and Brad Dourif, explores themes of authority, freedom, and individualism, with sharp critiques of institutional control. Shot in an actual psychiatric hospital in Oregon, the film received widespread acclaim and became only the second movie to win all five major Academy Awards, including Best Picture, Best Actor, and Best Actress. Despite some mixed reviews on its heavy-handed metaphors, it is now considered one of the greatest films ever made. Its unsettling score, atmospheric direction, and powerful performances contribute to its lasting impact. In 1993, the film was selected for preservation in the National Film Registry. "One Flew Over the Cuckoo's Nest" remains a cultural touchstone, with references in television and film, solidifying its place in cinematic history.

Shampoo

Shampoo

"Shampoo", released in 1975 and directed by Hal Ashby, stars Warren Beatty as George, a promiscuous Beverly Hills hairdresser who juggles relationships with several women, including those played by Julie Christie, Goldie Hawn, and Lee Grant. Set on Election Day 1968, the film explores the sexual politics and social mores of the late 1960s as George navigates his tangled personal life while dreaming of opening his own salon.

Co-written by Beatty and Robert Towne, the film satirizes both gender dynamics and the superficiality of Los Angeles culture. George's relationships with his clients, girlfriend, and ex-lover lead to increasingly complicated and chaotic situations.

Critically, "Shampoo" was well-received, with many praising its sharp writing and strong performances, though some, like Roger Ebert, found it disappointing. Commercially, it was a huge success, grossing over $60 million worldwide against a $4 million budget, making it the third-highest-grossing film of the year. The film remains a notable satire of 1960s America, capturing the changing dynamics of the era.

Top 1975 Movies at The Domestic Box Office (thenumbers.com)

Rank	Title	Release Date	Gross
1	Jaws	Jun 20, 1975	$260,000,000
2	One Flew Over the Cuckoo's Nest	Nov 19, 1975	$108,981,275
3	Shampoo	Feb 14, 1975	$49,407,734
4	Dog Day Afternoon	Aug 29, 1975	$46,665,856
5	The Return of the Pink Panther	May 16, 1975	$41,833,347
6	Three Days of the Condor	Sep 19, 1975	$41,509,797
7	Funny Lady	Mar 7, 1975	$40,055,897
8	The Rocky Horror Picture Show	Sep 26, 1975	$39,026,400
9	The Other Side of the Mountain	Nov 21, 1975	$34,673,100
10	Tommy	Mar 14, 1975	$34,251,525

The Rocky Horror Picture Show

Other Film Releases

From eccentric musical horrors to the bleak dystopian future, 1975 offered an unforgettable array of films that, while overlooked at the time, would later carve out their own legendary status. While box-office giants dominated headlines, a select group of underappreciated gems slipped through the cracks, only to be embraced as cult favorites in the years to come. Among them are six iconic films: "The Rocky Horror Picture Show," "Monty Python and the Holy Grail," "Picnic at Hanging Rock," "Barry Lyndon," "Deep Red," and "Rollerball."

Leading the charge is "The Rocky Horror Picture Show," a film whose blend of rock 'n' roll, horror, and campy humor revolutionized midnight movie culture. Initially considered a flop, it became a cultural phenomenon through fan participation, costume events, and sing-alongs. To this day, it's the quintessential cult film, with shadow casts and screenings still drawing audiences decades later.

"Monty Python and the Holy Grail" also found its place in cult history, thanks to its surreal and absurd brand of humor. The British comedy troupe's outrageous take on the Arthurian legend became a sleeper hit, and its relentless stream of quotable lines and memorable gags continues to captivate audiences worldwide. It's a film whose absurdity has only grown in esteem, inspiring generations of fans and filmmakers alike.

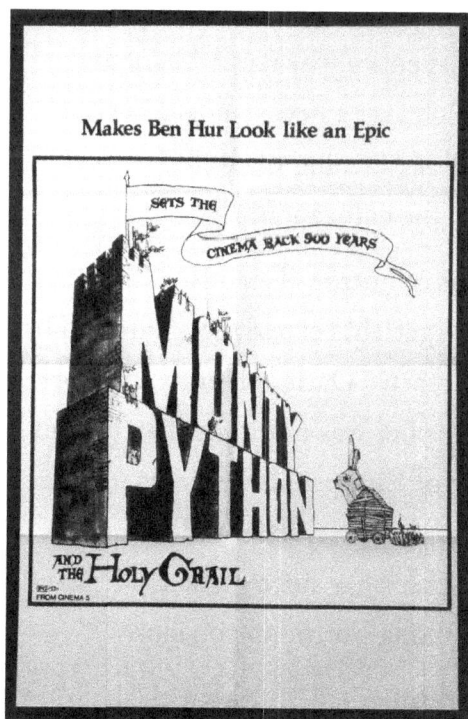

Monty Python and the Holy Grail

Picnic at Hanging Rock

Peter Weir's haunting mystery, "Picnic at Hanging Rock," offered something entirely different–an atmospheric, slow-burn thriller steeped in mystique. Although initially overshadowed by other films, its enigmatic plot and dreamlike visuals transformed it into a cult favorite. The unresolved nature of its central mystery has kept viewers intrigued for decades, sparking countless theories about the film's meaning.

"Barry Lyndon," Stanley Kubrick's sweeping historical drama, may have confounded audiences with its deliberate

Barry Lyndon

pacing and meticulous attention to detail, but over time, it has become revered as one of the director's finest works. The film's stunning cinematography,

Deep Red

lit almost entirely by natural light and candlelight, set a new standard in visual storytelling, earning it a well-deserved place in the cult canon.

For fans of horror, "Deep Red" delivered an unforgettable experience. Directed by Italian master Dario Argento, this gory giallo thriller was not immediately a hit outside of Europe. However, its unique blend of suspense, style, and inventive death scenes has since made it a beloved entry among horror aficionados.

Lastly, "Rollerball" offered a bleak vision of the future, where a violent sport

serves as a metaphor for societal control. Its dystopian themes resonated with sci-fi fans, who have come to appreciate its cautionary tale about the dangers of corporate power and unchecked violence. Today, it stands as a cult classic in the realm of 1970s science fiction.

Rollerball

Each of these films, in its own unique way, pushed boundaries and defied expectations, finding lasting appreciation in the hearts of devoted fans.

The 32nd Golden Globe Awards - Saturday, January 25th, 1975

🏆 Winners

Best Performance in a Motion Picture – Drama – Actor:
Jack Nicholson (Chinatown)

Best Performance in a Motion Picture – Drama - Actress:
Gena Rowlands (A Woman Under the Influence)

Best Performance in a Motion Picture
– Comedy or Musical – Actor:
Art Carney (Harry and Tonto)

Best Performance in a Motion Picture –
Comedy or Musical – Actress:
Raquel Welch (The Three Musketeers)

Best Supporting Performance in a Motion
Picture – Drama, Comedy or Musical –
Actor: Fred Astaire (The Towering Inferno)

Best Supporting Performance in a Motion
Picture – Drama, Comedy or Musical –
Actress: Karen Black (The Great Gatsby)

Best Director: Roman Polanski
(Chinatown)

Best Screenplay: Robert Towne
(Chinatown)

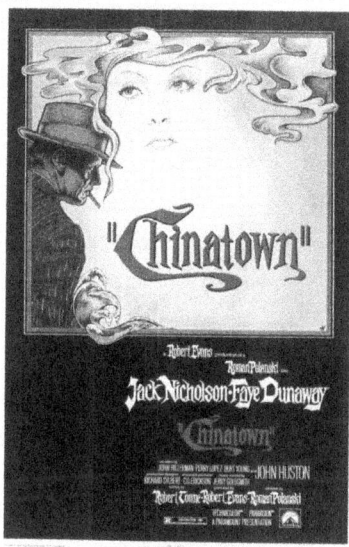

Best Motion Picture – Drama:
Chinatown

Best Motion Picture – Comedy or Musical:
The Longest Yard

The 28th British Academy Film Awards - Wednesday, February 26th, 1975

♆ Winners

Best Film: Chinatown (Roman Polanski)

Best Direction: Roman Polanski
(Chinatown)

Best Actor: Jack Nicholson
(Chinatown & The Last Detail)

Best Actress: Joanne Woodward
(Summer Wishes, Winter Dreams)

Best Supporting Actor: John Gielgud
(Murder on the Orient Express)

Best Supporting Actress: Ingrid Bergman
(Murder on the Orient Express)

Best Screenplay: Robert Towne
(Chinatown)

The 47th Academy Awards - Tuesday, April 8th, 1975 - Dorothy Chandler Pavilion, Los Angeles, California

Best Actor in a Leading Role:
Art Carney (Harry and Tonto)

Best Actress in a Leading Role: Ellen
Burstyn (Alice Doesn't Live Here Anymore)

Best Supporting Actor:
Robert De Niro (The Godfather Part II)

Best Supporting Actress: Ingrid Bergman
(Murder on the Orient Express)

Best Director:
Francis Ford Coppola
(The Godfather Part II)

Best Music (Song):
Al Kasha and Joel Hirschhorn
("We May Never Love Like This Again")

Best Cinematography:
Joseph Biroc (left picture) and Fred J. Koenekamp (right picture, in the center)
(The Towering Inferno)

Best Picture: The Godfather Part II

Top of the Charts

In 1975, music continued to evolve in exciting and diverse ways. Disco music exploded onto the mainstream, becoming synonymous with vibrant nightlife and flashy fashion. Bands like Earth, Wind & Fire and Donna Summer dominated the dance floors. Meanwhile, punk rock simmered beneath the surface, with bands like the Ramones offering a raw, rebellious counterpoint to the polished sound of disco. Progressive rock remained influential, with acts like Pink Floyd pushing musical boundaries. Additionally, the emergence of early hip hop in the Bronx laid the foundation for a genre that would soon reshape music culture globally. 1975 was a year where genres collided, giving voice to an increasingly multifaceted musical landscape.

Top Album: "Wish You Were Here" by Pink Floyd

Wish You Were Here

"Wish You Were Here", released in 1975, is the ninth studio album by Pink Floyd and is widely considered one of their finest works. The album was born out of sessions at London's EMI Studios, exploring themes of alienation and the music industry's corruption. Its standout track, "Shine On You Crazy Diamond," pays tribute to the band's troubled ex-member Syd Barrett, who made a surprise visit during its recording. The album, which also features the iconic tracks "Have a Cigar" and "Wish You Were Here," initially received mixed reviews but has since garnered universal acclaim. It sold over 13 million copies worldwide and remains a favorite among both fans and band members. Today, "Wish You Were Here" is celebrated as one of the greatest albums in progressive rock history.

Best Albums and Singles

In 1975, music reached new heights with a blend of rock, storytelling, and pop sensations. Bruce Springsteen's "Born to Run" became an anthem

Born to Run

Blood on the Tracks

Physical Graffiti

A Night at the Opera

Captain Fantastic & The Brown Dirt
Cowboy

for dreamers, while Bob Dylan's reflective "Blood on the Tracks" offered introspection. Led Zeppelin rocked with "Physical Graffiti", a double album of raw energy and intricate soundscapes, while Queen's "A Night at the Opera" dazzled with its operatic rock, featuring the legendary "Bohemian Rhapsody." Elton John also captivated with

"Captain Fantastic & The Brown Dirt Cowboy", and Fleetwood Mac's self-titled album marked a new chapter in their history.

On the singles chart, Captain & Tennille's "Love Will Keep Us Together" became the year's biggest hit, with Glen Campbell's "Rhinestone Cowboy" riding high.

Fleetwood Mac

Love Will Keep Us Together

Rhinestone Cowboy

Philadelphia Freedom

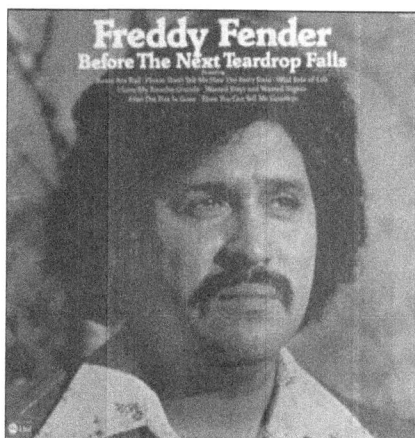

Before the Next Teardrop Falls

Elton John's "Philadelphia Freedom" brought pop brilliance, while Freddy Fender touched hearts with "Before the Next Teardrop Falls." Music in 1975 blended emotion, spectacle, and unforgettable melodies.

🎵 Top Albums 1975 (tsort.info):

1. Pink Floyd - Wish You Were Here
2. Bruce Springsteen - Born To Run
3. Bob Dylan - Blood On The Tracks
4. Led Zeppelin - Physical Graffiti
5. Queen - A Night At The Opera
6. Elton John - Captain Fantastic & The Brown Dirt Cowboy
7. Fleetwood Mac - Fleetwood Mac
8. Wings - Venus & Mars
9. Paul Simon - Still Crazy After All These Years
10. Eagles - One Of These Nights

🎵 Top Singles 1975 (billboardtop100of.com):

1. Captain and Tennille - Love Will Keep Us Together
2. Glen Campbell - Rhinestone Cowboy
3. Elton John - Philadelphia Freedom
4. Freddy Fender - Before The Next Teardrop Falls
5. Frankie Valli - My Eyes Adored You
6. Earth, Wind and Fire - Shining Star
7. David Bowie - Fame
8. Neil Sedaka - Laughter In The Rain
9. Eagles - One Of These Nights
10. John Denver - Thank God I'm A Country Boy

The 17th Annual Grammy Awards - March 1st, 1975 - Uris Theatre - New York

🏆 Winners

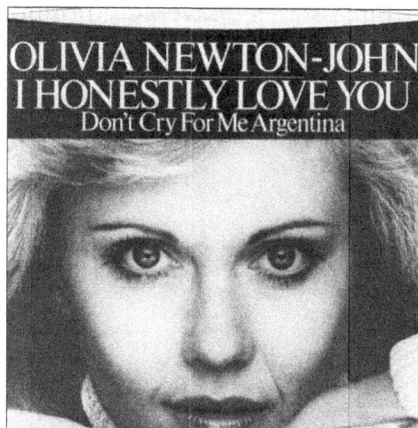

Record of the Year: John Farrar (producer) & Olivia Newton-John for "I Honestly Love You"

Album of the Year: Fulfillingness' First Finale – Stevie Wonder

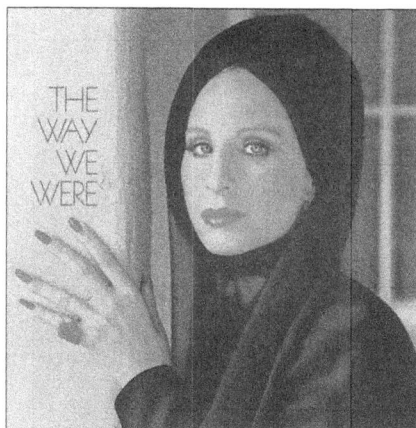

The Way We Were

Best New Artist: Marvin Hamlisch

Television

In 1975, American and UK television saw major shifts. Groundbreaking shows like Saturday Night Live and Wheel of Fortune in the U.S. transformed entertainment formats, while drama series delivered emotional moments that resonated with audiences. Game shows and live comedy sketches reached new levels of popularity. In the UK, with BBC and ITV

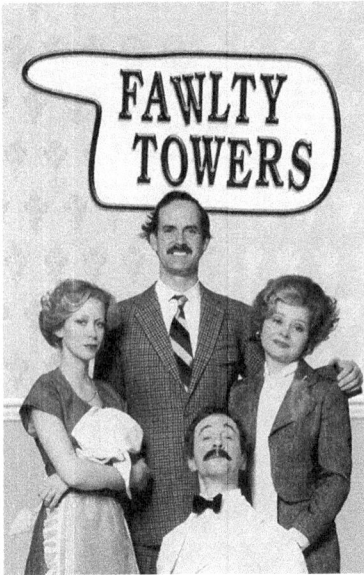

Fawlty Towers

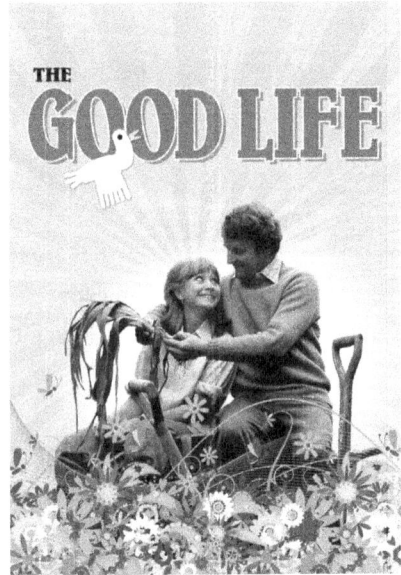

The Good Life

leading the way, "Fawlty Towers" and "The Good Life" brought iconic British humor into homes, cementing their cultural influence. Across both countries, TV in 1975 reflected broader societal shifts, blending new formats with a mix of humor, drama, and innovative storytelling.

Original "Jeopardy!" Ends After 11 Years - January 3rd

After an 11-year run, the original "Jeopardy!" came to a close, marking the end of an era for the beloved quiz show. Created by Merv Griffin and hosted by Art Fleming, the show flipped the traditional game show format, with

Jeopardy

contestants providing questions to given answers. Although it ended, the show's impact was lasting, leading to revivals and the iconic version hosted by Alex Trebek from 1984 until his death in 2020. Today, with Ken Jennings as the host, "Jeopardy!" remains one of television's most enduring and acclaimed quiz shows.

"Wheel of Fortune" Premieres - January 6th

"Wheel of Fortune", created by Merv Griffin, premiered with a format where contestants solve word puzzles to win cash and prizes by spinning a carnival wheel. Originally hosted by Chuck Woolery and Susan Stafford, it quickly gained popularity. Over time, Pat Sajak and Vanna White became the iconic hosts, leading the show into an enduring success. Today, "Wheel of Fortune" is the longest-running syndicated game show in U.S. television history, with international adaptations and millions of loyal viewers worldwide.

Wheel of Fortune

McLean Stevenson's Shocking Exit on "M*A*S*H" - March 18th

McLean Stevenson's departure from "M*A*S*H" shocked fans, as his character, Lt. Colonel Henry Blake, met a tragic end. Originally cast in a supporting role, Stevenson felt constrained by the ensemble format and sought to leave for better opportunities. His final episode saw Blake discharged, only to be killed in a plane crash–an unexpected and emotional twist for both the cast and viewers. Stevenson's exit left a significant impact on the series, and he was replaced by Harry Morgan as Colonel Sherman Potter.

M*A*S*H

"Alice Cooper: The Nightmare" Airs on ABC - April 25th

"Alice Cooper: The Nightmare" was a groundbreaking television special that brought the dark, theatrical world of Cooper's Welcome to My Nightmare album to life. Airing on ABC, it followed the story of "Steven," played by Cooper, as he is trapped in a surreal nightmare from which he cannot escape. The special also featured legendary horror actor Vincent Price as the "Spirit of the Nightmare." Combining rock music with a haunting narrative, it solidified Cooper's place in the world of shock rock.

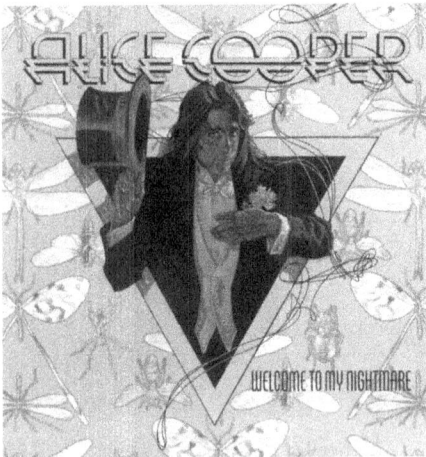

Alice Cooper: The Nightmare

John Lennon's Last TV Interview: "The Tomorrow Show" - April 28th

John Lennon's interview on The Tomorrow Show with Tom Snyder offered fans a rare glimpse into his personal and professional life. During this in-depth conversation, Lennon reflected on his post-Beatles

John Lennon and host Tom Snyder

life, the band's influence, and the challenges he faced, including potential deportation from the U.S. He shared candid thoughts on The Beatles' success, Ringo Starr's solo career, and his own calmer, post-Beatlemania lifestyle. Following Lennon's tragic death in 1980, the interview became a poignant and treasured moment in television history.

"Saturday Night Live" Debuts on NBC - October 11th

Saturday Night Live

The debut of Saturday Night Live on NBC brought a new form of live, late-night sketch comedy to American television. Created by Lorne Michaels, the show became famous for its edgy humor, parodying American culture and politics. The first episode featured comedian George Carlin as host, setting the tone for a format that would include celebrity hosts, musical performances, and a cold open sketch. Over time, SNL launched the careers of numerous comedians and became an enduring television institution.

Television Ratings 1975 (classic-tv.com)

1974-75 Shows

Rank	Show	Estimated Audience
1	All in the Family	20,687,000
2	Sanford and Son	20,276,000
3	Chico and The Man	19,522,500
4	The Jeffersons	18,906,000
5	M*A*S*H	18,769,000
6	Rhoda	18,015,500
7	Good Times	17,673,000
8	The Waltons	17,467,500
9	Maude	17,056,500
10	Hawaii Five-O	16,988,000

1975-76 Shows

Rank	Show	Estimated Audience
1	All in the Family	20,949,600
2	Rich Man, Poor Man	19,488,000
3	Laverne & Shirley	19,140,000
4	Maude	17,400,000
5	The Bionic Woman	17,330,400
6	Phyllis	17,052,000
7	Sanford and Son	16,982,400

8	Rhoda	16,982,400
9	The Six Million Dollar Man	16,912,800
10	ABC Monday Night Movie	16,843,200

The 32nd Golden Globe Awards - Saturday, January 25th, 1975

Winners

Best Drama Series: Upstairs, Downstairs

Best Musical/Comedy Series: Rhoda

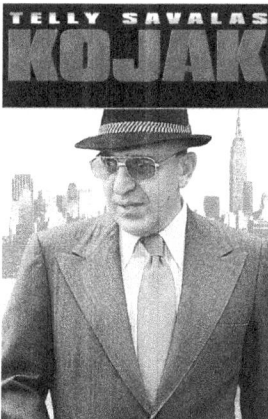

Best Actor - Drama Series:
Telly Savalas (Kojak)

Best Actress - Drama Series: Angie
Dickinson (Police Woman)

Best Actor - Musical/Comedy Series: Alan
Alda (M*A*S*H)

Best Actress - Musical/Comedy Series:
Valerie Harper (Rhoda)

Best Supporting Actor in a Series,
Miniseries or Television Film:
Harvey Korman (The Carol Burnett Show)

Best Supporting Actress in a Series,
Miniseries or Television Film:
Betty Garrett (All in the Family)

Chapter IV: Sports Review 1975

American Sports

Super Bowl Triumph: Steelers Take the Title - January 12th

Super Bowl IX saw the Pittsburgh Steelers secure their first-ever championship by defeating the Minnesota Vikings 16-6. Both teams were defensive powerhouses, with future Hall of Fame quarterbacks Terry Bradshaw and Fran Tarkenton at the helm. The game's first

Vikings' quarterback down in the end zone after a safety sack by Dwight White

half was a defensive standoff, highlighted by the first safety in Super Bowl history. Franco Harris led the Steelers with a record 158 rushing yards and a touchdown, earning him MVP honors. Despite injuries, Pittsburgh's defense dominated, limiting the Vikings to just 119 total offensive yards and no offensive touchdowns.

Benny Parsons: Daytona 500's Fastest - February 16th

The 1975 Daytona 500 saw Benny Parsons claim his first victory in this iconic race, outlasting both fierce competition and an unprecedented crash that took out nearly a quarter of the field. David Pearson had a commanding lead late in the race but was spun out after contact with Cale Yarborough, allowing Parsons to capitalize on the incident and take the checkered flag. Richard Petty

Benny Parsons inside his winning car

also played a key role by partnering with Parsons in a draft to close the gap. Ultimately, Parsons' strategic driving and luck helped secure his spot as Daytona's fastest.

Golden State Warriors Conquer NBA Championship - May 25th

The Golden State Warriors stunned the basketball world by sweeping the Washington Bullets in the NBA Finals to claim their first championship in eight years. Despite being underdogs, the Warriors, led by star forward Rick Barry and coached by Al Attles, dominated the heavily favored Bullets. Barry was named Finals MVP for his standout performance. The series also made history by featuring two black head coaches—Attles and K.C.

Warriors' George Johnson (52) and Rick Barry (24) double-team Hayes to block his shot

Jones. Playing some games at the Cow Palace due to venue conflicts, the Warriors secured their place in NBA history with a 4-0 series win.

King's Court: Chris Evert's US Open Victory - September 7th

Chris Evert claimed her first US Open title by defeating Evonne Goolagong in a thrilling final. After losing the first set 5-7, Evert bounced back to win the next two sets 6-4, 6-2, securing her fourth major

Chris Evert

singles title overall. This victory marked a turning point in her career after four consecutive semifinal finishes. It was also the first year the tournament was played on clay courts, adding a new challenge to the competition. Evert's win cemented her place among tennis greats, showcasing her resilience and skill on the grand stage.

The Reds Secure MLB World Series Title: October 22nd

Members of the Cincinnati Reds'
'Big Red Machine' team

The 1975 World Series, the 72nd edition of the championship, pitted the Cincinnati Reds against the Boston Red Sox in one of baseball's most iconic matchups. The Reds secured the title with a 4-3 series win, marking their first championship in 35 years.

Game 6 became legendary due to Carlton Fisk's dramatic walk-off home run, forcing a decisive Game 7. In the final game, the Reds rallied from a 3-0 deficit to win 4-3, with Joe Morgan's ninth-inning single sealing the victory. Pete Rose was named Series MVP, batting .370 across the series.

British Sports

Derby County: Football League Champions - April 29th

Derby County: Football League Champions

Derby County claimed their second Football League title in four years, overcoming fierce competition from Liverpool, Ipswich Town, Everton, and others in a thrilling season. Managed by Dave Mackay, Derby's triumph came down to the wire in one of the closest title races in history. Sheffield United, despite their strong campaign, fell short, while Carlisle United, making their debut in the top flight, were relegated after a promising start. Manchester United, managed by Tommy Docherty, returned to the First Division, winning the Second Division. The 1974-75 season was marked by intense battles, surprising turns, and a shifting landscape in English football.

West Ham United Claims FA Cup - May 3rd

West Ham United triumphed in the 94th FA Cup, defeating Fulham 2-0 in the final at Wembley. It marked West Ham's second FA Cup victory, with both goals scored by Alan Taylor, making him the hero of the match.

Fulham, a Second Division side at the time, made an impressive run to the final but couldn't overcome West Ham's determined performance. The game was broadcast live on both BBC and ITV, drawing millions of viewers. The 1974-75 FA Cup season also included several dramatic replays, showcasing the excitement and unpredictability that the competition is known for.

West Ham United team celebrates their victory

First Cricket World Cup Held in England - June 7th-21st

The West Indies Team

The 1975 Cricket World Cup, known as the Prudential Cup '75, was the inaugural men's Cricket World Cup, taking place in England from June 7 to 21. Eight teams participated, including the six Test-playing nations: Australia, England, India, New Zealand, Pakistan, and the West Indies, plus Sri Lanka and East Africa. The matches were played in a 60-over format, with West Indies emerging victorious against Australia by 17 runs in the final at Lord's. Clive Lloyd's stunning century (102) led the West Indies to a total of 291/8. Australia chased valiantly, but ultimately fell short. This historic tournament marked the beginning of One Day International (ODI) cricket as a major global event.

Ashe Conquers: Wimbledon's Men's Singles Champion - July 5th

Arthur Ashe made history by defeating defending champion Jimmy Connors in a stunning Wimbledon men's singles final, winning 6-1, 6-1, 5-7, 6-4. This victory marked Ashe's first Wimbledon singles title and his third and final major singles

Arthur Ashe hoists the trophy

championship. By claiming this title, Ashe became the first Black man to win Wimbledon, and only the second Black player overall, following Althea Gibson. Ashe, who was seeded sixth, played a tactical match, using precision and strategy to outmaneuver the top-seeded Connors, securing his place as a trailblazer in tennis history.

International Sports

Soviet Glory: Ice Hockey World Title - April 19th

The 1975 Ice Hockey World Championships, held in West Germany, saw the Soviet Union dominate the tournament, securing their 14th World Championship title and 17th European title. Playing in Munich and Düsseldorf, the Soviet team proved unstoppable, winning all 10 of their games with an impressive 90 goals scored and only 23 conceded. Czechoslovakia took the silver, while Sweden clinched the bronze, leaving Finland in fourth place yet again. Despite being anticipated to deliver, the tournament lacked much drama, as the expected rankings prevailed, and host West Germany didn't compete in the top tier. This predictable outcome eventually led to changes in player eligibility and tournament format.

Soviet Union National Ice Hockey Team

Thévenet Triumph: Tour de France Winner - July 20th

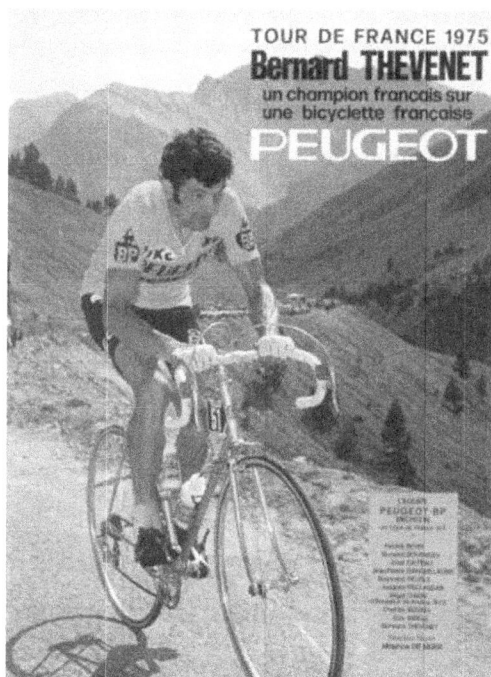

Bernard Thévenet

The 62nd Tour de France saw Bernard Thévenet triumph, ending Eddy Merckx's quest for a sixth consecutive win. Despite starting strong, Merckx faced unforeseen challenges, including being punched by a spectator and later suffering a fall that resulted in a broken cheekbone. These setbacks allowed Thévenet to seize the lead and ultimately win, with Merckx finishing second. Belgian riders dominated other categories, with Rik Van Linden taking the points classification, Lucien Van Impe winning the mountains classification, and Marc Demeyer excelling in intermediate sprints. The first young rider classification was introduced, won by Italy's Francesco Moser.

Despite his loss, Merckx's resilience in continuing the race despite injuries remains legendary.

Speed Mile: Walker Sets World Record - August 12th

New Zealand's John Walker made history by becoming the first person to run the mile in under 3 minutes and 50 seconds, clocking an impressive 3:49.4 in Göteborg, Sweden. This achievement shattered the previous

John Walker

world record of 3:51.0 set by Tanzania's Filbert Bayi earlier that year. Walker's milestone occurred 21 years after Roger Bannister's famous sub-four-minute mile and earned him the title of Athlete of the Year by Track and Field News. His remarkable feat remained unbeaten until 1979, cementing his legacy as one of middle-distance running's greatest athletes.

Ali Conquers: Thrilla in Manila Victory - October 1st

Muhammad Ali and Joe Frazier inside the boxing ring

The "Thrilla in Manila," the third and final bout between Muhammad Ali and Joe Frazier, remains one of boxing's most iconic battles. Held at the Araneta Coliseum in the Philippines, Ali won after Frazier's corner conceded following the 14th round. This brutal contest, known for its intensity, pushed both fighters to their limits, with Ali famously describing it as the closest he'd felt to dying. The event also marked a milestone in sports broadcasting, as Home Box Office became the first pay television network to deliver a continuous satellite signal, making this high-stakes match accessible to a wider audience. With an estimated 1 billion viewers, the fight cemented Ali's legacy as heavyweight champion.

Chapter V: General 1975

Pop Culture

"The Wiz" Opens on Broadway - January 5th

"The Wiz," a contemporary African-American retelling of "The Wonderful Wizard of Oz," opened on Broadway and became an iconic cultural milestone. With music and lyrics by Charlie Smalls and a book by William F. Brown, it marked one of Broadway's first mainstream productions featuring an all-Black cast. Initially receiving mixed

The Wiz on Broadway

reviews, it gained momentum, partly thanks to a TV ad campaign. The show won seven Tony Awards, including Best Musical, and ran for four years, influencing future African-American Broadway hits.

John Lennon

John Lennon Wins Deportation Battle - October 7th

After a four-year battle, John Lennon won his deportation case against the U.S. government, securing his right to remain in the country. Targeted for his anti-Vietnam War stance, the government used a 1968 marijuana conviction to try to deport him. The landmark ruling stated that the conviction wasn't grounds for deportation, allowing Lennon to seek permanent residency. This victory was followed by the birth of his son, Sean, just two days later. In 1976, Lennon received his green card, granting him official residency status.

David Bowie Becomes the "Thin White Duke" - 1975 (Exact Date Unknown)

David Bowie

David Bowie introduced his "Thin White Duke" persona, an enigmatic and controversial character that became synonymous with his 1976 album "Station to Station." The Duke, influenced by Bowie's role in "The Man Who Fell to Earth," sported slicked-back blonde hair, cabaret-style clothing, and exuded an air of detachment. Known for his chilling and emotionless demeanor, the Duke attracted controversy due to seemingly pro-fascist remarks. Bowie later disavowed these comments, attributing them to heavy drug use and stating they didn't reflect his true beliefs.

Bill Clinton Marries Hillary Rodham - October 11th

Bill Clinton and Hillary Rodham tied the knot in a small Methodist ceremony in their Fayetteville living room. Despite the traditional expectations of the time, Hillary chose to retain her maiden name, becoming Hillary Rodham instead of Clinton. Her decision was driven by a desire

Bill Clinton and Hillary Rodham
on their wedding dress

to keep her professional identity, maintain individuality, and avoid conflicts of interest, which initially upset both mothers. This marriage marked the beginning of a partnership that would become one of the most famous political alliances in American history.

Stephen King Releases "Salem's Lot" - October 17th

Stephen King's second published novel, 'Salem's Lot, introduced readers to a chilling tale set in the small town of Jerusalem's Lot, Maine, where residents mysteriously turn into vampires. The story follows writer Ben Mears as he confronts the evil lurking in his hometown. Praised for its haunting atmosphere and terrifying plot, the novel earned nominations for the World Fantasy Award and the Locus Award. Later adapted into two miniseries, 'Salem's Lot solidified King's reputation as a master of horror storytelling.

Salem's Lot

Bohemian Rhapsody

Queen Releases "Bohemian Rhapsody" - October 31st

Queen's "Bohemian Rhapsody" was released as a lead single from their album A Night at the Opera and quickly became a groundbreaking hit, topping the UK charts for nine weeks. Despite its unconventional length and structure, the song blended opera, rock, and ballad elements, establishing Queen's reputation for musical innovation. Initially, their label resisted releasing it, but radio DJ Kenny Everett's enthusiastic airplay generated overwhelming demand. Now considered one of the greatest rock songs ever, it propelled Queen to international stardom.

Most Popular Books from 1975 (goodreads.com)

- ⭐ 'Salem's Lot - Stephen King
- ⭐ Tuck Everlasting - Natalie Babbitt
- ⭐ Shōgun (Asian Saga, #1) - James Clavell
- ⭐ Factotum - Charles Bukowski
- ⭐ The Philosophy of Andy Warhol (From A to B and Back Again) - Andy Warhol
- ⭐ Strega Nona - Tomie dePaola
- ⭐ Forever... - Judy Blume
- ⭐ Discipline and Punish: The Birth of the Prison - Michel Foucault

* Danny the Champion of the World - Roald Dahl

* The Miracle of Mindfulness: An Introduction to the Practice of Meditation - Thich Nhat Hanh

* Crocodile on the Sandbank (Amelia Peabody, #1) - Elizabeth Peters

* Where Are the Children? (Where Are the Children, #1) - Mary Higgins Clark

* Ragtime - E.L. Doctorow

* Ramona the Brave (Ramona, #3) - Beverly Cleary, Alan Tiegreen (Illustrator)

Technological Advancements

Altair 8800 Microcomputer Released - January 1975

The release of the Altair 8800 microcomputer in January marked a monumental shift in personal computing. Designed by MITS and powered

Altair 8800 Microcomputer

Office lady using the Altair 8800 Microcomputer

by the Intel 8080 CPU, it captured public interest after appearing on the cover of Popular Electronics. As the first commercially successful personal computer, the Altair 8800 sparked the microcomputer revolution and introduced the S-100 bus, establishing a foundational standard in early computing. Significantly, Altair BASIC became Microsoft's inaugural product, launching its journey in software development. This groundbreaking machine inspired countless enthusiasts and laid the essential groundwork for the modern PC industry, transforming how we interact with technology today.

Monoclonal Antibodies Discovered by Milstein and Köhler - August 7th

César Milstein and Georges Köhler

César Milstein and Georges Köhler made a groundbreaking scientific leap on August 7th by discovering how to produce monoclonal antibodies, a technique published in Nature. They combined mouse spleen cells with myeloma cells, creating a hybridoma capable of generating large amounts of antibodies with a single specificity. Initially overlooked, this breakthrough transformed biomedical research, enabling precise diagnostics and targeted therapies for numerous diseases. Their discovery profoundly impacted medical science and led to numerous therapeutic applications. In recognition of their work, Milstein and Köhler were awarded the Nobel Prize in Physiology or Medicine in 1984, alongside Niels Jerne, cementing their legacy in modern medicine.

Lyme Disease First Recognized in Connecticut - 1975 (Exact Date Unknown)

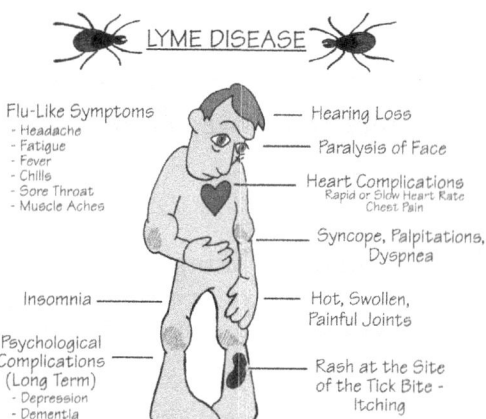

Lyme Disease illustrated

In 1975, a mysterious cluster of arthritis cases in Lyme, Connecticut, led to the identification of Lyme disease. By 1977, scientists linked the disease to bites from the black-legged tick (Ixodes scapularis). The bacterium Borrelia burgdorferi was pinpointed in 1982 as the causative agent, marking a critical breakthrough in understanding this illness. Despite public health efforts, Lyme disease remains a significant issue, with approximately 30,000 cases diagnosed annually in Connecticut. Ongoing surveillance, education, and prevention strategies aim to control its spread, but the disease continues to challenge healthcare systems, emphasizing the importance of continued research and awareness in combating this growing public health threat.

Wallace Broecker

"Global Warming" Term Coined by Broecker - August 8th

Wallace Broecker, a geochemist, introduced the term "global warming" into scientific discourse, signaling a groundbreaking moment in climate science. Known as Wally, Broecker's research focused on the impact of human carbon dioxide emissions on rising Earth temperatures. His work mapped global ocean circulation, emphasizing its influence on climate change. Broecker's journey to this insight began with carbon dating studies at Columbia University's Lamont-Doherty Earth Observatory. Despite initial skepticism, his prediction about temperature rises proved pivotal, earning him recognition as a climate change prophet.

NASA Launches Viking 1 to Mars - August 20th

NASA's Viking 1 mission marked a major achievement in space exploration as it became the first spacecraft to land successfully on Mars. Launched on August 20th via a Titan/Centaur vehicle, it reached Mars after an 11-month journey. Originally planned for a July 4th touchdown, the landing was delayed due to rough terrain and ultimately occurred on July 20th, 1976, exactly seven years after Apollo 11. Viking 1's lander conducted pioneering biology experiments to detect signs of life, producing intriguing but inconclusive results. While some experiments suggested possible life, others indicated chemical reactions,

The Titan III-Centaur carrying the Viking 1 Lander lifted off on August 20, 1975

Sunset of Mars as photographed by Viking 1

fueling ongoing debate. Viking 1's mission set the stage for future Mars exploration and operated for over six years.

Sasson Creates First Portable Digital Camera - December 1975

Steven J. Sasson holding the first portable digital camera he created

In December, Steven J. Sasson, an electrical engineer at Kodak, revolutionized photography by creating the first portable digital camera. Weighing 8 pounds (3.6 kg), this groundbreaking device used a Fairchild CCD image sensor with a resolution of 100 × 100 pixels (0.01 megapixels) and captured images in black and white. Each photo was stored digitally on a cassette tape, taking 23 seconds per image. Despite being a prototype, it was the first self-contained, hand-held digital camera. Kodak patented the invention in 1977, recognizing its innovative "electronic still camera" technology. Sasson's creation laid the foundation for the digital photography era, transforming how images would be captured and stored in the future.

Fashion

Fashion in 1975 was a dynamic continuation of the trends that defined the early 1970s, yet it also introduced a more tailored and layered approach. This year saw a preference for high-quality fabrics like Harris tweed, wool flannel, cashmere, camel's hair, pure cotton, and pure silk, reflecting an emphasis on texture and craftsmanship.

In 1975, women embraced a blend of feminine and utilitarian styles. The wrap dress, popularized by Diane von Fürstenberg, continued to be a

How guys dressed in the 70s

staple, combining professional appeal with evening glamour. An increased use of pastel colors and Asian patterns marked this year, alongside suede coats, peacoats, blazers, cowl-neck sweaters, and tube dresses, which became wardrobe standards. Floral patterns were especially prominent, as seen in popular fashion

70s outfits for women

70s Floral Patterns

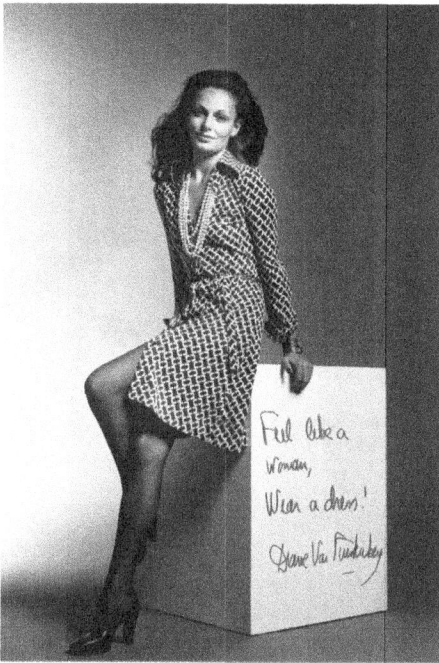

Diane von Furstenberg in her iconic
wrap dress

magazines like *Harper's Bazaar*. Layering remained significant, with women often wearing multiple blouses, sweaters, or dresses paired with trousers or tunic dresses. The jumpsuit emerged as a key activewear trend, with flared legs and varying sleeve lengths, often completed with sneakers and tennis headbands to capture the growing athletic lifestyle. Meanwhile, the influence of disco was evident in the rise of sequined halter tops, spandex shorts, and flared trousers that shimmered on the dance floor.

70s Jumpsuits

Flared trousers

70s Men's Fashion

Men's fashion in 1975 drew inspiration from European tailoring, resulting in the quasi-European suit characterized by slightly padded shoulders, higher armholes, prominent waist suppression, and a light flare to both jacket and pants. Accessories like oversized collars added disco glamor to more conservative styles. Denim jackets, corduroy sport jackets, and plaid combinations in polyester-rayon blends reflected the balance between comfort and formality. Shoes adopted a flamboyant tone, with platform

70s Men's Style

heels reaching up to 3 inches, and vibrant color schemes appearing in both men's and women's footwear. Accessories remained minimal, with simple gold neck chains serving as a unisex staple. Women favored wedge-heeled espadrilles, knee-high boots, and platform shoes, while men's footwear took on bolder designs. Iconic aviator glasses also became a signature accessory, worn by influential figures like Gloria Steinem.

In essence, 1975's fashion was a captivating fusion of global influences, blending utility with glamor. The interplay of comfort, vintage inspirations, and modern flair made 1975 a memorable year in fashion history, leaving an indelible mark on the era's style.

Cars

The car industry in 1975 was significantly shaped by the aftermath of the 1973 oil crisis. This resulted in fuel-efficient cars gaining a larger market share, with the Energy Policy and Conservation Act introducing the Corporate Average Fuel Economy (CAFE) standards, which pushed manufacturers to prioritize efficiency in their designs. As a result, there was a notable shift toward smaller, more economical vehicles, even though car prices increased substantially in 1975 due to changing equipment and features.

Top Selling Cars

U.S.A

1975 Oldsmobile Cutlass

The Oldsmobile Cutlass took the crown as the best-selling car in the U.S., with 324,610 units sold. This marked a significant rise from its previous ranking, showing that American consumers still valued domestic brands despite fuel efficiency concerns. The

1975 Ford Granada

Ford Granada made an impressive debut with 291,140 units sold, capturing second place. The Chevrolet Chevelle remained popular, ranking third with 276,206 units sold, followed closely by the Ford Pinto, last year's top seller, which sold 271,880 units. Other notable performers included the Chevrolet Monte Carlo, which reached 267,803 units, and the Chevrolet Nova, which maintained strong sales at 256,438 units. In addition, the AMC Pacer, a unique and distinctive model, made its mark with 88,641 units, showing a trend toward more compact and unconventional designs.

U. K.

In the United Kingdom, the Ford Cortina maintained its dominance, selling approximately 129,000 units in 1975. It continued to be a symbol of British automotive reliability and comfort, even amid the ongoing recession. The Ford Escort, another staple in the UK market, sold around 100,000 units, solidifying its position as a popular choice for small families. These

1975 Ford Cortina

1975 Ford Escort

sales figures highlighted Ford's stronghold in the UK market, showing that despite economic challenges, consumers still preferred Ford's blend of affordability, style, and performance.

Fastest Car

The 1975 Ferrari 308 GTB/ GTS stood out as one of the fastest and most notable cars of the year, representing Ferrari's transition from the Dino series. The 308 GTB came in both coupe and targa (GTS) body styles and featured a naturally

1975 Ferrari 308 GTB/GTS

aspirated mid-engined V8 engine, setting a new standard for luxury sports cars. This model's adaptability and raw performance earned it a place in automotive history, and it later evolved into the 328 series in the mid-1980s.

Most Expensive Car Sold in America in 1975

The Mercedes-Benz 450 SEL 6.9 was one of the most luxurious and expensive cars of 1975. Although it wasn't an American brand, it set a high standard for luxury vehicles sold in the U.S. The 450 SEL was equipped with a powerful V8 engine and had features that were considered ahead of its time, such as hydropneumatic suspension and advanced safety features. With a price tag of around $15,000, it outclassed many domestic competitors and became a status symbol for luxury and refinement, showcasing the shift toward more sophisticated, technologically advanced vehicles.

1975 Mercedes-Benz 450 SEL 6.9

Most Powerful Muscle Car of 1975

1975 Chevrolet Monza 2+2

The muscle car era was in decline during this time due to stricter emission controls and rising fuel prices. However, some models managed to capture enthusiasts' attention. The Chevrolet Monza 2+2, often considered part of the sports car category rather than a traditional muscle car, offered a glimpse into the evolving American performance car landscape. Although not as powerful as earlier muscle cars, the Monza was a standout with its compact design and sporty characteristics. The focus was on agility and handling rather than sheer power, reflecting changing consumer preferences and regulatory pressures.

In conclusion, 1975 marked a pivotal year for the automotive industry, with shifts toward fuel efficiency, luxury, and a blend of performance that responded to economic challenges and changing consumer demands. This year highlighted how automakers adapted to an evolving market, balancing tradition with innovation.

Popular Recreation

Disco on the Dance Floor

In 1975, leisure and recreation continued to capture the evolving cultural landscape. Disco's influence remained strong, but it wasn't the only source of excitement. Songs like "Love Will Keep Us Together" by The Captain and Tennille topped the charts, becoming an anthem, while Queen's "Bohemian Rhapsody," which was particularly successful in the UK, started making waves, becoming a staple at social gatherings and parties.

As disco filled dance floors, indoor activities offered different forms of escapism. Dungeons & Dragons gained even more enthusiasts, with players immersing themselves in epic adventures, fostering social interaction, teamwork, and storytelling. The game became a popular pastime, uniting friends and families around tables to explore fantasy realms, and gained notable popularity in both the U.S. and UK.

Television also remained central to leisure activities. Shows like

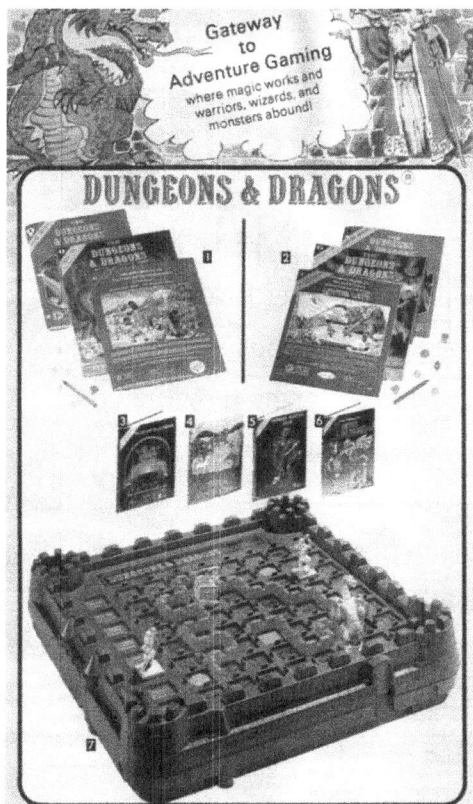

Dungeons & Dragons

"All in the Family" continued to entertain American audiences, while in the UK, viewers enjoyed a mix of American imports and local programs. New hits like "Laverne & Shirley" and "The Six Million Dollar Man" gained widespread popularity, drawing families together and often sparking discussions beyond the screen.

Pet Rock

In 1975, toys and games left a memorable mark on pop culture. The "Pet Rock" became an unexpected phenomenon in the U.S., showing how even the simplest ideas could capture the public's interest. Meanwhile, action figures based on "The Six Million Dollar Man" became essential for many kids, tapping into the growing appeal of television-inspired toys. The introduction of the home version of "Pong," one of the

1975 Vintage Six Million Dollar Man

Home version of Pong

earliest video games, marked a significant moment, ushering in a new era of electronic entertainment for children and adults alike.

Across the UK and the U.S., classic board games like "Risk," "Monopoly," and "Connect Four" continued to be popular, encouraging strategic thinking and friendly rivalries among family and friends.

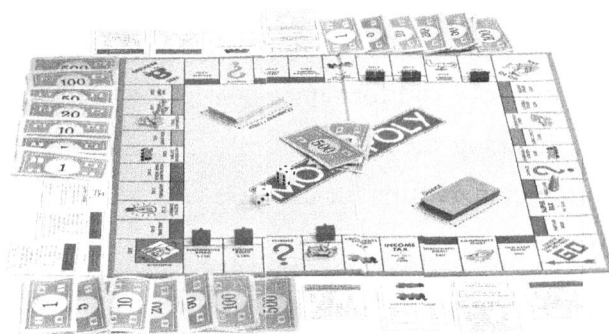

Monopoly

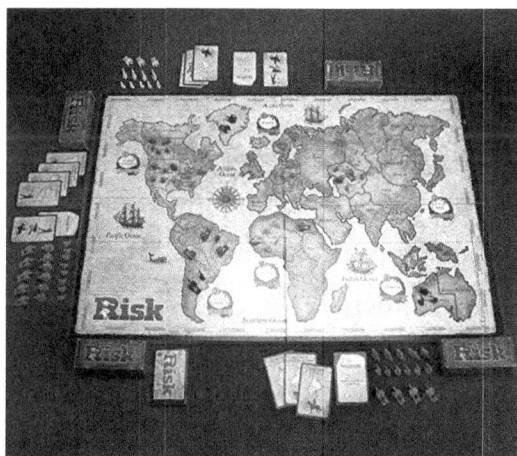

Risk Game

Connect Four

These games fostered shared experiences, providing hours of fun at home and during social gatherings. Mood rings, which changed color based on body temperature, added a touch of novelty and fashion, encapsulating the playful spirit of the mid-70s.

Outdoor activities also saw a surge in popularity. Cycling gained momentum, driven by increased environmental awareness, a trend that was especially strong in the UK, where it became a widely embraced leisure activity. Roller-skating rinks evolved into social hubs, providing spaces for people to gather, exercise, and enjoy the latest music hits. Leisure suits, often made from polyester, were the go-to fashion choice, offering both comfort and style, making them perfect for dancing, skating, or casual outings.

Cycling in the 70s

Movies played a significant role in 1975's leisure scene, with "Jaws" becoming a blockbuster hit that captured audiences worldwide. More than just a cinematic experience, the film became a cultural phenomenon, even influencing how people viewed beach outings. In the UK, while "Jaws" was widely popular, "Monty Python and the Holy Grail" stood out as a comedy classic, quickly becoming a beloved part of British pop culture. Drive-in theaters thrived in the U.S., offering an affordable and enjoyable way to watch films under the stars.

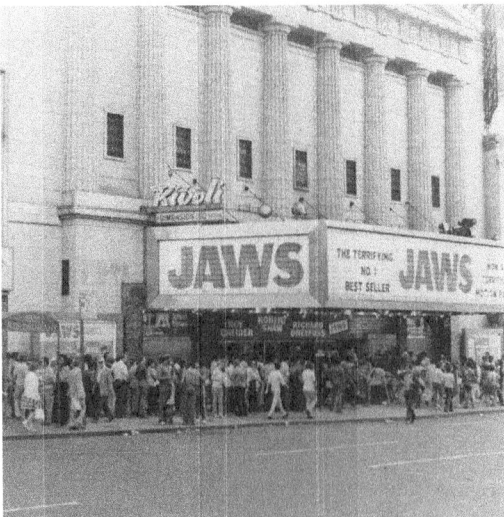

Jaws, when it first came out in 1975

Overall, 1975 was a year of transition, with leisure activities serving as both a means of escape and a way to connect. From disco's energy to the more relaxed enjoyment of board games, the year captured a rich mix of entertainment, interaction, and the pursuit of fun, marking a vibrant chapter in the history of popular recreation on both sides of the Atlantic.

Chapter VI: Births & Deaths 1975

Births (onthisday.com)

January 5th – Bradley Cooper: American Actor and Filmmaker

February 22nd – Drew Barrymore: American Actress

March 15th – Eva Longoria: American Actress and Producer

March 27th – Fergie: American Pop Singer

April 2nd – Pedro Pascal: Chilean-American Actor

April 10th – David Harbour: American Actor

April 14th – Anderson Silva: Brazilian-American Mixed Martial Artist

May 2nd – David Beckham: British Soccer Player

May 3rd – Christina Hendricks: American Actress

May 8th – Enrique Iglesias: Spanish Singer

May 26th – Lauryn Hill: American Rapper and Singer

May 27th – Andre 3000: American Rapper

May 29th – Mel B: British Singer

June 4th – Angelina Jolie: American Actress

June 4th – Russell Brand: British Comedian and Actor

June 7th – Allen Iverson: American Basketball Player

June 25th – Linda Cardellini: American Actress

June 27th – Tobey Maguire: American Actor

July 6th – 50 Cent: American Rapper

August 7th – Charlize Theron: South African-American Actress

August 16th – Taika Waititi: New Zealand Filmmaker, Actor, and Comedian

September 4th – Mark Ronson: British-American Music Producer

September 9th – Michael Bublé: Canadian Jazz Singer

September 18th – Jason Sudeikis: American Actor and Comedian

September 25th – Declan Donnelly: British TV Show Host

September 30th – Marion Cotillard: French Actress

October 5th – Kate Winslet: British Actress

October 22nd – Jesse Tyler Ferguson: American TV Actor

October 25th – Antony Starr: New Zealand TV Actor

November 14th – Travis Barker: American Drummer

November 26th – DJ Khaled: American Music Producer

December 13th – Tom DeLonge: American Rock Singer

December 17th – Milla Jovovich: Ukrainian-American Actress and Supermodel

December 18th – Sia: Australian Pop Singer

December 27th – Heather O'Rourke (1975-1988): American Child Actress

December 30th – Tiger Woods: American Golfer

Deaths (onthisday.com)

February 14th – P. G. Wodehouse: English Author and Humorist

March 14th – Susan Hayward: American Actress, Academy Award winner

March 15th – Aristotle Onassis: Greek Shipping Magnate

March 25th – Faisal of Saudi Arabia: King of Saudi Arabia

April 10th – Marjorie Main: American Actress, "Ma and Pa Kettle"

April 14th – Fredric March: American Actor, two-time Oscar winner

April 15th – Richard Conte: American Actor, "The Godfather"

April 17th – Sarvepalli Radhakrishnan: 2nd President of India

April 19th – Percy Lavon Julian: American Chemist, steroid pioneer

April 24th – Pete Ham: Welsh Singer-Songwriter

June 3rd – Ozzie Nelson: American Actor, Bandleader

June 4th – Evelyn Brent: American Film and Stage Actress

June 19th – Sam Giancana: American Mobster, Chicago Outfit boss

August 8th – Cannonball Adderley: American Jazz Saxophonist

August 15th – Sheikh Mujibur Rahman: Founding Father of Bangladesh

August 29th – Éamon de Valera: Former President of Ireland

September 29th – Casey Stengel: American Baseball player/manager

October 2nd – K. Kamaraj: Chief Minister of Tamil Nadu

October 30th – Martha Moxley: American Murder victim

November 2nd – Pier Paolo Pasolini: Italian Filmmaker, Poet

November 4th – Sheila Ryan: American Film Actress

December 1st – Anna Roosevelt Halsted: American Writer, Roosevelt's daughter

Chapter VII: Statistics 1975

GDP

* ✶ U.S. GDP 1975 – 1.68 trillion USD (worldbank.org)
* ✶ U.S. GDP 2023 – 27.36 trillion USD (worldbank.org)
* ✶ U.K. GDP 1975 – 241.76 billion USD (worldbank.org)
* ✶ U.K. GDP 2023 – 3.34 trillion USD (worldbank.org)

Inflation

* ✶ U.S. Inflation 1975 – 9.1% (worldbank.org)
* ✶ U.S. Inflation 2023 – 4.1% (worldbank.org)
* ✶ U.K. Inflation 1975 – 24.2% (worldbank.org)
* ✶ U.K. Inflation 2023 – 6.8% (worldbank.org)

Population

* ✶ U.S. Population 1975 – 215,973,000 (worldbank.org)
* ✶ U.S. Population 2023 - 334,914,895 (worldbank.org)
* ✶ U.K. Population 1975 – 56,225,800 (worldbank.org)
* ✶ U.K. Population 2023 - 68,350,000 (worldbank.org)

Life Expectancy at Birth

* ✶ U.S. Life Expectancy at Birth 1975 - 73 (worldbank.org)
* ✶ U.S. Life Expectancy at Birth 2022 – 77 (worldbank.org)
* ✶ U.K. Life Expectancy at Birth 1975 – 73 (worldbank.org)
* ✶ U.K. Life Expectancy at Birth 2022 – 82 (worldbank.org)

Annual Working Hours Per Worker

* ✶ U.S. Annual Working Hours Per Worker 1975 - 1,812 (ourworldindata.org)

* U.S. Annual Working Hours Per Worker 2017 - 1,757 (ourworldindata.org)
* U.K. Annual Working Hours Per Worker 1975 - 1,814 (ourworldindata.org)
* U.K. Annual Working Hours Per Worker 2017 - 1,670 (ourworldindata.org)

Unemployment Rate

* U.S. Unemployment Rate 1975 – 8.2% (thebalancemoney.com)
* U.S. Unemployment Rate 2023 – 3.6% (worldbank.org)
* U.K. Unemployment Rate 1975 - 5.1% (ons.gov.uk)
* U.K. Unemployment Rate 2023 – 4.0% (ons.gov.uk)

Tax Revenue (% of GDP)

* U.S. Tax Revenue (% of GDP) 1975 – 16.4% (ceicdata.com)
* U.S. Tax Revenue (% of GDP) 2022 – 12.2% (worldbank.org)
* U.K. Tax Revenue (% of GDP) 1975 – 33.3% (ceicdata.com)
* U.K. Tax Revenue (% of GDP) 2022 – 27.3% (worldbank.org)

Prison Population

* U.S. Prison Population 1975 - 240,593 (bjs.ojp.gov)
* U.S. Prison Population 2021 - 1,230,100 (bjs.ojp.gov)
* U.K. Prison Population 1975 - 37,000 (parliament.uk)
* U.K. Prison Population 2023 - 97,700 (parliament.uk)

Average Cost of a New House

* U.S. Average Cost of a New House 1975 – $42,600 (dqydj.com)
* U.S. Average Cost of a New House 2023 – $495,100 (dqydj.com)
* U.K. Average Cost of a New House 1975 – £10,388 (ons.gov.uk)
* U.K. Average Cost of a New House 2023 – £290,000 (ons.gov.uk)

Average Income per Year

* U.S. Average Income per Year 1975 – $13,778.73 (multpl.com)
* U.S. Average Income per Year US 2023 – $106,400 (multpl.com)
* U.K. Average Income per Year 1975 – £3,000 (parliament.uk)
* U.K. Average Income per Year 2023 – £34,963 (parliament.uk)

U.S. Cost of Living

* U.S. Cost of Living: The $100 from 1975 has grown to about $585.12 today, up $485.12 over 49 years due to an average yearly inflation of 3.67%, resulting in a 485.12% total price hike (in2013dollars.com).

U.K. Cost of Living

* U.K. Cost of Living: Today's £1,051.29 mirrors the purchasing power of £100 in 1975, showing a £951.29 hike over 49 years. The pound's yearly inflation rate averaged 4.92% during this period, leading to a 951.29% total price rise (in2013dollars.com).

Cost Of Things

United States

* Men's sport coats: $30.00 - $55.00 (mclib.info)
* Men's shirts, Arrow: $6.00 - $12.00 (mclib.info)
* Women's pant suits, polyester: $10.99 (mclib.info)
* Fresh eggs (1 dozen): $0.77 (stacker.com)
* White bread (1 pound): $0.36 (stacker.com)
* Sliced bacon (1 pound): $1.29 (mclib.info)
* Round steak (1 pound): $1.89 (stacker.com)
* Potatoes (10 pounds): $0.99 (mclib.info)
* Fresh grocery milk (1/2 gallon): $0.79 (stacker.com)

- ★ Coffee, Chock Full O'Nuts (1 lb can): $0.99 (mclib.info)
- ★ Apples, McIntosh (3 lbs): $0.59 (mclib.info)
- ★ Butter, Hotel Bar (1 lb): $0.70 (mclib.info)
- ★ Beef, ground chuck (1 pound): $0.99 (mclib.info)
- ★ Beans, baked, Campbell's (1 lb can): $0.24 (mclib.info)
- ★ Soup, Campbells (5 cans): $1.00 (mclib.info)
- ★ Ketchup, Heinz (26-ounce bottle): $0.59 (mclib.info)

United Kingdom (retrowow.co.uk)

- ★ Gallon of petrol: 73p
- ★ Bottle of whisky (Haig) (Key Markets): £3.39
- ★ Pint of beer: 28p
- ★ Pint of milk: 7p
- ★ Large loaf of bread: 15p
- ★ 22" Ultra colour TV (Currys): £259.00
- ★ 20" Ferguson black & white TV (Currys): £74.95
- ★ Daily Mirror newspaper: 5p
- ★ ½lb Lurpack butter (Safeway): 14p
- ★ Nescafé 4oz coffee (Tesco): 35p
- ★ Can of Coke (Tesco): 7½p
- ★ Hotpoint Supermatic twin tub washing machine (Currys): £122.95
- ★ Indesit fridge-freezer (Currys): £109.95
- ★ One dozen large white eggs: 38p
- ★ 1lb Stork soft margarine (Key Markets): 20p
- ★ Jacobs Cream Crackers (Sainsbury's): 13p

Chapter VIII: Iconic Advertisements of 1975

Budweiser

Armstrong's Quaker Rugs

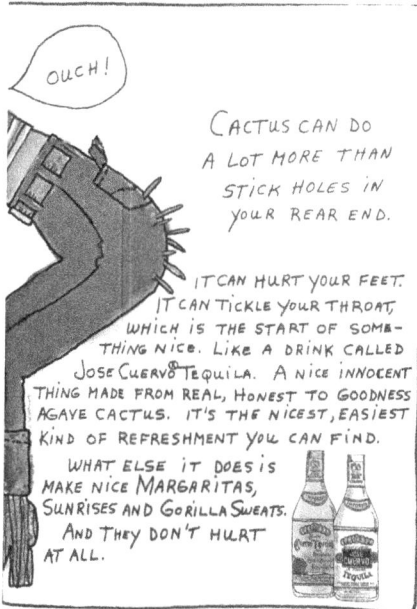

Jose Cuervo Tequila

Palmolive

Coca-Cola

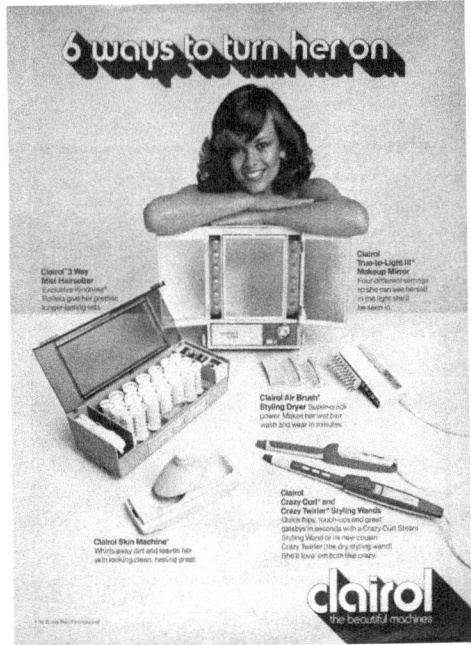

Clairol Beauty Products

1975 Ford Mustang II

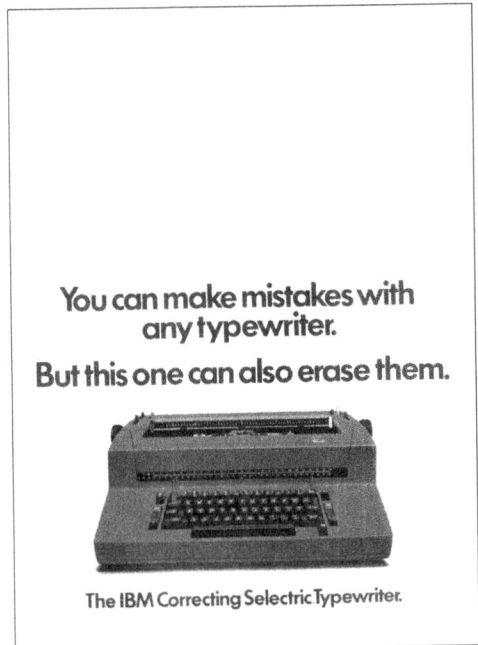

IBM Correcting Selectric Typewriter

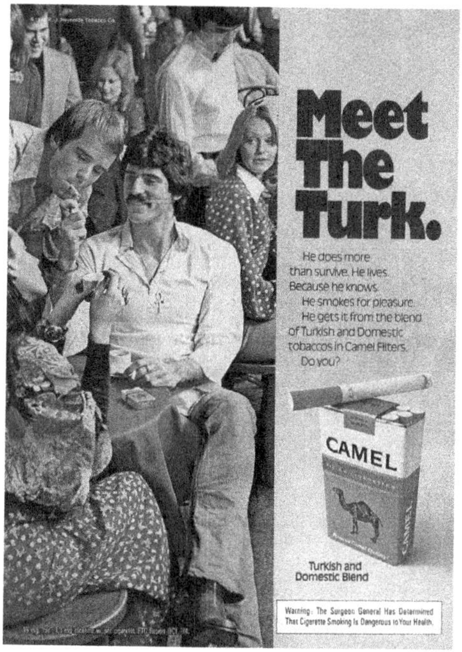

Camel

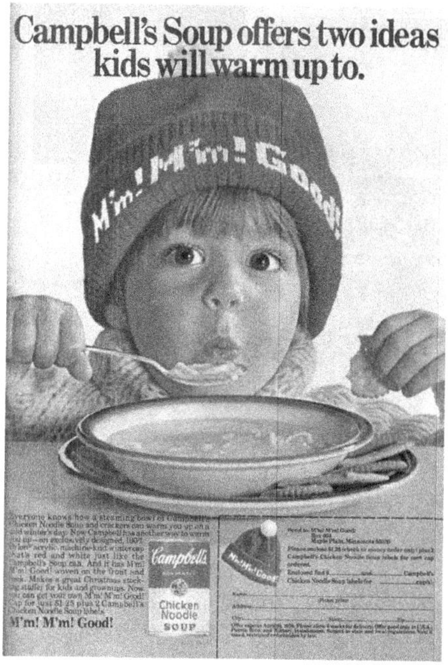

Campbell's Soup

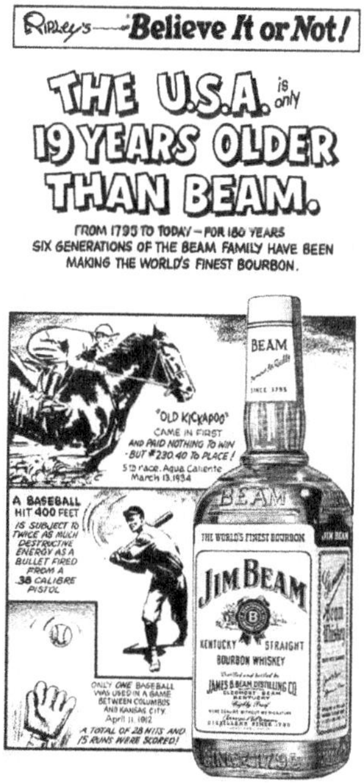

Jim Beam

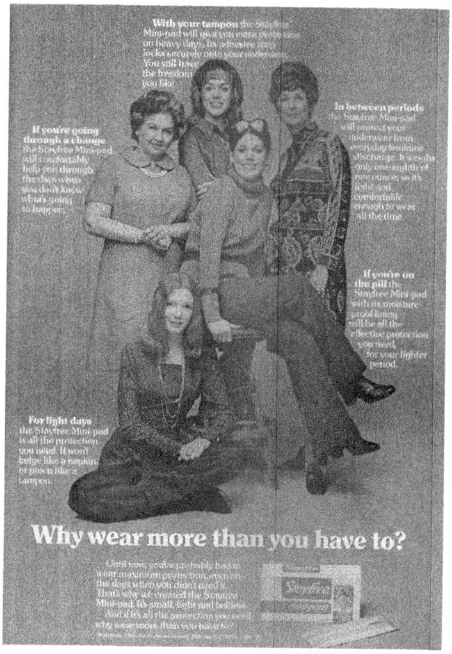

Stayfree Mini-pads

From a brilliant past... a brilliant present.

Announcing Cadillac 1975. As responsive to the needs of today's luxury car owner as was the 1938 Cadillac Town Car in its day. With better overall operating economy than its efficient 1974 counterpart. With an array of standard features unsurpassed in Cadillac history. With new features available... like the Astroroof. New excitement. New efficiency. New value. Then and Now... on American Standard for the World.

Cadillac '75

Cadillac '75

PHILIPS

Phillips

You've come a long way, baby.

VIRGINIA SLIMS

Virginia Slims

Kellogg's PRODUCT 19

The high-nutrition cereal with that good Kellogg's taste.

It just makes good common sense to start your breakfast with a bowl of Kellogg's® Product 19® It gives you 100% of the U.S. Recommended Daily Allowance of ten vitamins and iron. In a crunchy blend of four wholesome grains. High nutrition and good taste. That's Kellogg's Product 19.

"It's the Common Sense Cereal."

Kellogg's Product 19

Who cares enough to make the world half as big by flying twice as fast?

We care!

The world's a smaller place with British Airways Concordes. Our supersonic flights cut hours off your flying times between London and New York, Washington, Dallas-Fort Worth, Bahrain and Singapore!

Now with our Concordes, you can have a late breakfast in Singapore and be in Dallas-Fort Worth for dinner!

You fly twice as fast, twice as high and arrive fresher, more relaxed, ready for work.

British Airways Concordes cut the world down to size - supersonically.

British airways
We'll take more care of you

British Airways

A fine addition to any penthouse, townhouse, triplex or estate.

For people who deny themselves nothing. Tanqueray Gin. A singular experience.

Tanqueray

To the rigors of training, we've brought the style of champions. Converse All Star Training shoes. They color the action.

International track shoe design, Converse All Star quality and three different styles. In suede or smooth leather with uppers of white, red, gold or blue combos to make a fine, tough, good looking athletic shoe for use in the most rigorous conditioning, warm-ups, jogging, calisthenics, or plain casual wear. See your Converse sporting goods dealer and let him show you these beautifully made, colorful training shoes.

★ converse ∙ Eltra

Selected for use by the U.S. team for the 1976 Olympic Games in Montreal.

Converse All Star Training Shoes

Isn't this too much tire to turn down?

1. The Proven Gas Saver This is the tire that earned the name Gas Saver. When run at steady highway speeds against our original equipment belted tires, use it saved up to thirty miles per tankful, important savings at today's gas prices!

2. 7 Day Test Ride and Handling Warranty We're so sure you'll like the smooth ride and quick, positive handling of the Steel Radial 500™ that you can buy them, drive on them for seven days, and get every cent back if there's anything you don't like. Does any other tire company offer you that?

3. 40,000 Mile Warranty If the Steel Radial 500 doesn't give you 40,000 miles of normal passenger use on the same car, any Firestone Dealer participating Dealer will give you a new one, charging you only for the mileage received plus Federal Excise Tax. A small service charge may be added.

4. New Water Squeezer Tread Firestone's unusual new Water Squeezer Tread actually pushes water out the sides of the tread to help keep water from getting between the rubber and the road. And the tough, Steel Radial 500 footprint puts a lot of tread under you to help hold tight to wet pavement.

5. Steel Between You and Tire Trouble Two belts of steel cord under the new Water Squeezer Tread help protect your tires from chuckholes and roadjunk* that you don't always steer around. They also hold the tread firmly to cut down on the "squirm" that causes wear.

*Don't forget—the safety of your tires is also affected by air pressure, wear, load, and operating conditions.

Firestone

New Firestone 40,000 mile Steel Radial 500

Firestone Steel Radial 500

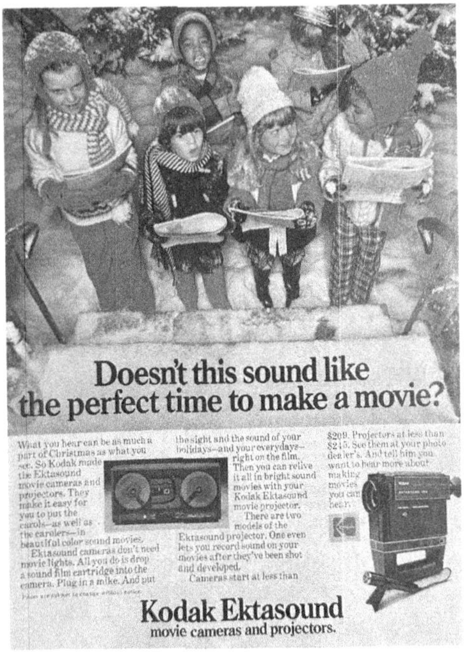

Kodak Ektasound

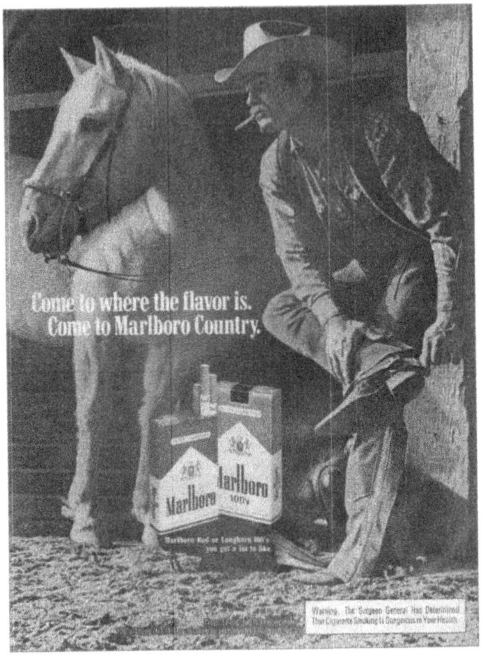

Marlboro

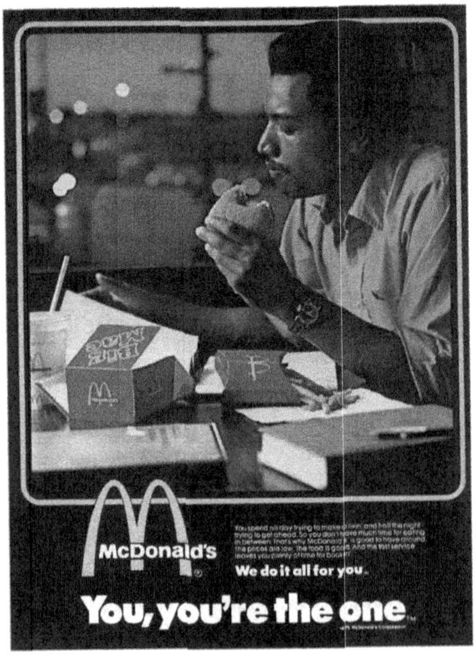

McDonald's

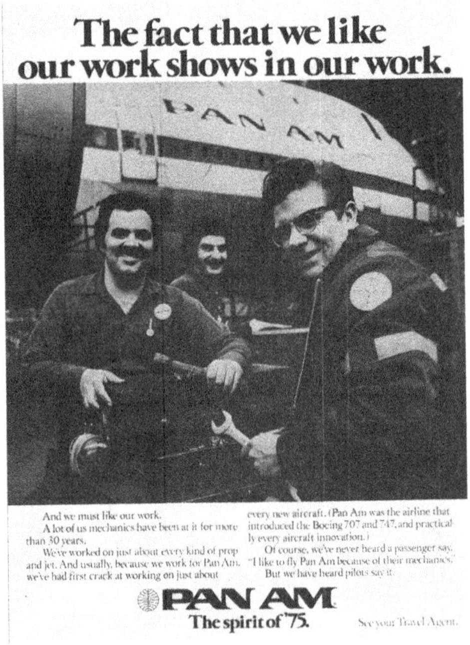

Pan Am

Gordon's

Tide

'75 Corvette

Sony Trinitron

Johnnie Walker Red

I have a gift for you!

Dear reader, thank you so much for reading my book!

To make this book more (much more!) affordable, all images are in black and white, but I've created a special gift for you!

You can now have access, for FREE, to the PDF version of this book with the original images!

Keep in mind that some are originally black and white, but some are colored.

I hope you enjoy it!

Download it here:

bit.ly/3ChVdpE

Or Scan this QR Code:

I have a favor to ask you!

I deeply hope you've enjoyed reading this book and felt transported right into 1975!

I loved researching it, organizing it, and writing it, knowing that it would make your day a little brighter.

If you've enjoyed it too, I would be extremely grateful if you took just a few minutes to leave a positive customer review and share it with your friends.

As an unknown author, that makes all the difference and gives me the extra energy I need to keep researching, writing, and bringing joy to all my readers. Thank you!

Best regards,
Alex J. Harper

Please leave a positive book review here:

https://amzn.to/48I5l6Z

Or Scan this QR Code:

Discover Other Books in this Collection!

TIME TRAVELING TO
1944
CELEBRATING A SPECIAL YEAR

Relive the Culture, the People, the Leading Events, and the Arts That Shaped 1944

TIME TRAVELING TO
1945
CELEBRATING A SPECIAL YEAR

Relive the Culture, the People, the Leading Events, and the Arts That Shaped 1945

TIME TRAVELING TO
1953
CELEBRATING A SPECIAL YEAR

Relive the Culture, the People, the Leading Events, and the Arts That Shaped 1953

TIME TRAVELING TO
1954
CELEBRATING A SPECIAL YEAR

Relive the Culture, the People, the Leading Events, and the Arts That Shaped 1954

TIME TRAVELING TO
1955
CELEBRATING A SPECIAL YEAR

Relive the Culture, the People, the Leading Events, and the Arts That Shaped 1955

TIME TRAVELING TO
1963
CELEBRATING A SPECIAL YEAR

Relive the Culture, the People, the Leading Events, and the Arts That Shaped 1963

TIME TRAVELING TO
1964
CELEBRATING A SPECIAL YEAR

Relive the Culture, the People, the Leading Events, and the Arts That Shaped 1964

TIME TRAVELING TO
1965
CELEBRATING A SPECIAL YEAR

Relive the Culture, the People, the Leading Events, and the Arts That Shaped 1965

TIME TRAVELING TO
1973
CELEBRATING A SPECIAL YEAR

Relive the Culture, the People, the Leading Events, and the Arts That Shaped 1973

TIME TRAVELING TO
1974
CELEBRATING A SPECIAL YEAR

Relive the Culture, the People, the Leading Events, and the Arts That Shaped 1974

TIME TRAVELING TO
1975
CELEBRATING A SPECIAL YEAR

Relive the Culture, the People, the Leading Events, and the Arts That Shaped 1975